Transgenerational Trauma and Therapy

Transgenerational Trauma and Therapy presents the transgenerational, psychological impacts of trauma, and the clinical work on it. The book's expansive insight explores the psychology of the massive, collective trauma, and provides new ways of understanding the serious after-effects of man-made suffering.

In this book, Bakó and Zana employ their original concept, "the transgenerational atmosphere", to fully comprehend many familiar phenomena in a new theoretical framework, exploring the psychological impact of trauma on the first generation, the mode of transmission, the effects on future generations, and therapeutic considerations. Crucially, *Transgenerational Trauma and Therapy* explores the psychological effects of collective, societal traumas on whole groups of individuals. Beginning with the direct, deep psychological effects of individual trauma, and then exploring the impact of collective trauma over generations, it deals particularly with the role of the social environment in the processing of trauma, as well as its hereditary transmission.

Rich in rich clinical material and methodological suggestions, *Transgenerational Trauma and Therapy* will appeal to mental health professionals, including psychiatrists, psychologists, psychoanalysts, and social workers, in addition to professors in other academic disciplines, such as sociology, history, philosophy, and anthropology.

Tihamér Bakó, PhD., is a Training and Supervising Analyst of the Hungarian Psychoanalytical Society (IPA) and Training and Supervising Psychodramatist of the Hungarian Psychodramatical Society. He works in a private practice in Budapest and is the author of several professional books in the areas of trauma, crisis, suicide, and supervision.

Katalin Zana, MD, PhD., is a psychotherapist and Candidate of the Hungarian Psychoanalytical Society (IPSO). She is the author of several publications in the areas of transgenerational trauma, narrative, and creativity, and works in a private practice in Budapest.

Transgenerational Trauma and Therapy

The Transgenerational Atmosphere

Tihamér Bakó and Katalin Zana

Routledge
Taylor & Francis Group

LONDON AND NEW YORK

First published 2020
by Routledge
2 Park Square, Milton Park, Abingdon, Oxon OX14 4RN

and by Routledge
52 Vanderbilt Avenue, New York, NY 10017

Routledge is an imprint of the Taylor & Francis Group, an informa business

British Library Cataloguing-in-Publication Data
A catalogue record for this book is available from the British Library

Library of Congress Cataloging-in-Publication Data
Names: Bakó, Tihamér, 1955- author. | Zana, Katalin, author.
Title: Transgenerational trauma and therapy : the transgenerational atmosphere / Tihamér Bakó, Katalin Zana.
Description: Abingdon, Oxon ; New York, NY : Routledge, 2020. | Includes bibliographical references and index.
Identifiers: LCCN 2019044822 (print) | LCCN 2019044823 (ebook) | ISBN 9780367859329 (hbk) | ISBN 9780367859312 (pbk) | ISBN 9781003015840 (ebk)
Subjects: MESH: Stress Disorders, Post-Traumatic–psychology | Stress Disorders, Post-Traumatic–therapy | Intergenerational Relations | Stress, Psychological–psychology | Psychotherapy
Classification: LCC RC552.T7 (print) | LCC RC552.T7 (ebook) | NLM WM 172.5 | DDC 616.85/21–dc23
LC record available at https://lccn.loc.gov/2019044822
LC ebook record available at https://lccn.loc.gov/2019044823

ISBN: 978-0-367-85932-9 (hbk)
ISBN: 978-0-367-85931-2 (pbk)
ISBN: 978-1-003-01584-0 (ebk)

Typeset in Times New Roman
by Swales & Willis, Exeter, Devon, UK

Printed and bound in Great Britain by
TJ International Ltd, Padstow, Cornwall

Contents

Reflections   90

Acknowledgments

We want to express our special thanks to all colleagues for their support and participation in the process of making this book.

Thanks to Andrea Sinkovics and Naomi V. Cutner for their careful and thorough specialist revision of the Hungarian and English texts, for their professional suggestions, for the useful advice and stimulating ideas that help us so much in giving final shape to the book.

Thanks to our translator Richard Robinson for his painstaking work.

Thanks to Katalin Sebes for her editing suggestions. We owe particular thanks to Nancy R. Goodman and Ferenc Erős, who wrote forewords for the book. These sensitive, understanding, thought-provoking words have further enriched the ideas expressed in the book.

Finally we wish to thank contributors from other professions, Júlia Hardy (family psychotherapist), Rita Horváth (literary scholar), Dezső Németh (cognitive psychologist), András Szécsényi (historian), Ágnes Zana (cultural anthropologist), and János Zana (control systems specialist) for their highly stimulating thoughts which introduce new aspects. The pieces by these writers reflect not only on the ideas suggested in our book, but continue their train of thought to open up new perspectives, and bring the book to life.

Forewords

Nancy R. Goodman: Inspiration: Growing the Mind

Nancy R. Goodman, Ph.D., is training and supervising analyst with the Contemporary Freudian Society, Washington DC, and the International Psychoanalytical Association (IPA).

Many views of burned out landscapes that contain the feel and after-effects of trauma appear in this book. After reading the manuscript the result is an opening of thought, creation of poetic language, and birthing of new concepts providing the symbolism needed when trauma is without and within. The "transgenerational atmosphere" and the "transgenerational transference and countertransference" are new ideas adding to our model of the mind and of treatment. They bring light to the darkness of trauma residing in the patient, the therapist, and the "here and now" of therapy process. Trauma can be received in many ways, directly into one's psyche, from one's parents, and from the societal surround. Each enters the mind taking one's breath away and each deserves the articulation appearing in the chapters of this book.

There is a heartbeat in the words and ideas we find here. In so many ways the writing and thinking of Katalin Zana and Tihamér Bakó bring inspiration where previously there was only the nothing of overwhelming terror and anxiety. As a psychoanalyst who conducts treatments and writes about *The Power of Witnessing* (2012) in regard to the Holocaust, I feel renewed hope about how I can untangle suffering and offer more to my patients. Readers of this volume will know better how to make it possible for minds to touch and to think together even when the history of despair and atrocity are present. The topic of unremitting trauma always gives pause because there is so much pain to endure. In the psychoanalytic research presented and the psychoanalytic treatments described, with full transference and countertransference significance, readers will be enthralled as communications reach across the traumatic abyss making human contact.

The writing of Tihamér Bakó and Katalin Zana is deep; that is, the reader notes that they are unwavering in listening to societal trauma, like the Holocaust, and to individual terrors uncovered in clinical encounters.

Reverberations of human experience appear on every page and hold truths which then provide support and cushioning so that the reader does not collapse nor fall into despair. We are held in place with care as we are carried through such topics as transgenerational transmissions, transference and countertransference, enactments, silence, collapse of time, shame (at knowing and not knowing), holding and containment, retreat, mentalization, and reverie. The language used is beautiful such as this description conveying the affect of being traumatized. "The hibernated state with which the traumatized individual tries to defend themselves, as we have seen, paradoxically preserves the experience of loss, making it permanent." We discover here vibrant metaphors used theoretically and clinically to convey what we have to know about trauma and transgenerational trauma. In my thinking and psychoanalytic research, I discover over and over that it is the use of metaphor (Goodman, 2018) between two people, between analyst and patient, that creates shared narratives for transmitting affects and resilience of mind that can now take place. There is a special process when the "dead places" in the mind (the overwhelming traumas) come into contact with another who is witnessing, resulting in an intersubjective meeting for growing a "living space" (Goodman, 2012).

In the psychoanalytic understanding of the mind, there is layering from all developmental phases and subjective history turns into a deep narrative. The exploration of trauma is also layered appearing in treatment through enactments, countertransference, and body sensations (Ellman and Goodman, 2017) to develop symbolic meaning taking on the trauma story and unconscious fantasies associated with it. Tihamér Bakó and Katalin Zana use in-depth clinical examples illustrating how the patient and therapist may first perceive body knowing to be translated into symbolic story. We are told by them that the baby who is ready to receive the breast, care and safety, along with the mother's reverie and then finds a nothing is hurt in its capacity to imagine, to fantasize. And, that this is true for the mind in general when the destruction of psychic helplessness abounds. Given this fact, this truth, this book is all the more remarkable because it restores creation of symbol and metaphor and imagining.

Developing new concepts, especially useful ones, is imagining and provides hope. The description of "the intergenerational atmosphere" provides a new strong scaffolding offering firm footing for comprehending transgenerational trauma. All psychotherapists will have a new space in their minds for addressing transference and countertransference phenomena and repetitions. With this learning comes the possibility of helping terrified frozen patients to give up the *we*-experience of belonging to the family carrying the silence. The clinical descriptions show unwaveringly how being stuck in a forever trauma atmosphere of traumatic transference and helpless countertransference is transformed with this new understanding.

Not only is the therapeutic work reaching across the internal barriers of the patient and analyst, but it is also taking on the holes in the historic narrative forbidding knowledge. I am grateful to discover their conceptualization of this connection and will be better able to see it in my own treatments and for teaching of therapy work with trauma. Therapists will welcome the renewal of momentum as the time-space dimensions come into being. Emerging from "the atmosphere" is renewal; the past is the past, the present is here and now, and the future can enter imagination and fantasy. The time-space dimensions of the mind produce containment with narrative. It takes courage to be in the claustrophobic asphyxiating space of intense forgotten trauma. Breathing is renewed through the pages of this book, another meaning of inspiration.

The Power of Witnessing: Reflections, Reverberations, and Traces of the Holocaust—Trauma and Psychoanalysis (ed. with Marilyn Meyers, Routledge, 2012).

Finding Unconscious Fantasy in Narrative, Trauma, and Body Pain (ed. with Paula Ellman, Routledge, 2017).

Finding Metaphor and Symbol for the Unbearable: A Trauma Museum of the "Terrible Real" and "Creative Representations" in Healing Trauma: The Power of Listening, (ed. Evelyn Jaffe Schreiber, IPBooks, 2018, pp.183–202).

Ferenc Erős

Ferenc Erős DSc., professor emeritus, Doctoral School of Psychology, University of Pécs, Hungary.

Tihamér Bakó and Katalin Zana's book deals with the effect of psychological traumas involving several generations, in terms not only of the traumatized subject, but also of the more immediate and broader groups surrounding him or her, and the whole of society. The basic idea of their book is that although the ones who are subject to trauma, be it genocide and war or domestic violence, are the individuals themselves, an entire community shares in their traumatic experience. As well as those immediately involved, the so-called "bystanders" and even the perpetrators and their descendants can become traumatized. Thus individual and community trauma are intertwined from the start, and the combined effect has a considerable effect on the life, psychological state, intersubjective and interpersonal relationships of the survivors, and even of future generations. The effect winds its way down the generations and shows up particularly dramatically if there is no social and historical processing of the traumas in terms of collective memory, or if such processing is incomplete. This situation gives rise to what the writers call the "transgenerational atmosphere", which is nothing other than the survivor's attempt to share the experience, to process the trauma, and to engage in a mourning process. The survivor draws his or her descendants into this atmosphere, and they become participants in and victims of the original trauma, just like the first-generation survivors. Instead of coherent stories, they receive a legacy of silence and pain, unsymbolized memories, and fragmentary narratives.

The concept and description of the transgenerational atmosphere is closely linked to the debates that have been ongoing for over one hundred years in fields close to psychology, and more recently in philosophy, history, and sociology, on what existential and diagnostic status psychological trauma actually has, and to what extent it has a right to be recognized. The syndromic nature of psychological trauma, which cannot be traced back either to immediate organic causes or to psychopathological states, was already recognized by late-nineteenth-century psychiatrists, and as a result in the 1880s under Bismarck the state of Prussia recognized that those suffering from traumatic neurosis (e.g. victims of workplace and transport accidents) were entitled to compensation in the form of an allowance. But it was psychoanalysis that first uncovered the reasons for psychological trauma and how it forms, with the work of Sigmund Freud, Sándor Ferenczi, Michael Balint and others. Ferenczi, who served as a military doctor throughout the First World War recognized that grievous social violence, and war, trigger a particular form of neurosis, hitherto barely known of. The syndrome of wartime neurosis known as shellshock demands to be recognized as psychological trauma in its own right, and thus requires genuine therapy, rather than some punishment disguised as treatment e.g. electric shocks (which the mainstream psychiatry of the time was predisposed to visit upon traumatized soldiers).

Yet the path was long from war neuroses and Ferenczi's groundbreaking work to the appearance of the issue of transgenerational trauma. After the Second World War, psycho-sciences began to deal very intensively with survivor syndrome, which included both the sufferings of soldiers and prisoners-of-war and the "civilian" survivors (those deported, enclosed in ghettos, refugees, etc.). A special problem was posed by the surviving victims of the Holocaust, the majority of whom lost not only their family, friends, home, and social support network, but had to shape a new life, a new personal and social identity, returning to the homeland from which they had been driven, or as a refugee, an émigré, finding a new homeland in a new country or continent. However, a "latency period" of several decades preceded the recognition of the true depth, the uniqueness of Holocaust trauma and the elemental effect it has on identity and memory, and the idea that the origin of and reason for trauma is primarily external violence, the terror exercised by the state and its authorities that leads to mass murder, rather than the individual psychopathological state of the survivors prior to the trauma. A crucial role in this recognition was played by Holocaust memoirs, interviews, witness accounts, psychotherapy case studies, which came increasingly into the public eye in the 1960s and 70s, and not least the various legal actions and trials, which demanded adequate material and moral compensation for the survivors from the German state.

When twenty or thirty years had passed, from the end of the 1960s, the second generation became self-aware, one that continued to bear the trauma of the parents, and at the same time made enormous effort to break the silence of their forefathers, to break the prohibitions and taboos that blocked the path to their knowing their own family history, and the sufferings their parents had endured.

The arrival of the second generation and the attempt at self-reflection inspired clinical, socio-psychological, and historical research into the transgenerational transfer of trauma, placed in the cultural and historical context of the problem of Holocaust trauma (together with other gravely traumatic events). This book by Tihamér Bakó and Katalin Zana shows what psychological and social obstacles there are to self-reflection, and to the transformation of inherited emotions, fears, and anxieties into a symbolic narrative. A basis for understanding this is provided by the "phantom theory" of Mária Török and Miklós Ábrahám, and the presentation, contextualization and application of this is perhaps the most important part of Bakó and Zana's book. Török and Ábrahám, who were themselves descendants of victims of the Holocaust in Hungary, believed that the "phantom" was an attendant to traumas, conflicts and secrets that had their origin not in the subject's own life history, but in the experiences of previous generations, and because of this could not be described with traditional Freudian categories of repression. The "phantoms" find their way out of "capsules", psychic "crypts" that lie inaccessible for generations, defying narration, their effect appearing in the form of inexpressible, prolonged, "cryptic" grief.

The theoretical analyses and clinical interpretations of Bakó and Zana show that it is this phantomization that sustains the transgenerational atmosphere, which today can envelop the third and fourth generations. The breaking of the transgenerational atmosphere and the transformation of the unsymbolized atmosphere into symbolic culture is managed with the help of postmemory. In the words of American researcher Marianne Hirsch, postmemory is "retrospective witnessing by adoption". It is a question of adopting the traumatic experiences – and thus also the memories – of others as experiences one might oneself have had, and of inscribing them into one's own life story. Thus the relationship with the oppressed and persecuted Other is a tool, and can be used as a model: just as I "remember" my parents' memories, so I can "remember" anyone else's sufferings. Postmemory is a "personal interpretation of history": witness by one who is absent, in the sense that the witness is absent not only spatially, but also temporally, from the location where the event happened. Postmemory makes it possible to symbolically transform traumatic experiences, to communicate them, and can become a source of creativity. Today we are witnessing the birth of a transgenerational culture. Postmemory, which has given birth to great works of art such as László Nemes's film *Son of Saul*, represents and bears witness to the present the traumas which proved to be unprocessable for preceding generations. Postmemory is also the "memory of the present", because it makes relevant, and thus susceptible to debate, issues such as culpability, victimhood, the relationship between perpetrator and victim, collaboration, identification with the aggressor, and problems of dehumanization.

It is to be hoped it will also stimulate scholarly discourse in other fields dealing with this topic.

Preface

This book has as its focus the psychological effects of large-scale social-historical traumas. Setting out from the direct deep psychological effects of individual trauma, and progressing towards the effect over generations of collective trauma, we deal particularly with the role of the social environment in the processing of trauma, and the hereditary transmission of trauma.

An accepting, safe, social environment, in the narrow and wider sense, which is able to understand and mirror the feelings of the other, is fundamentally important not only in early relationships for the formation of a healthy personality, but is necessary throughout one's entire life, in order for the personality to continue to function healthily. The model we propose attempts to interpret the group processes within a psychoanalytical framework; in other words, we examine how familiar concepts such as mirroring and containing can help us to understand the interaction of individual and group processes. Simultaneously with this we assume that psychological processes at the individual level cannot be interpreted without an understanding of group-level events, in other words of the broader social milieu, and whether or not it can contain, has an effect on the early development of the individual. The birth of the sovereign self, capable of symbolization and mentalization, is dependent on the container capacity not merely of the early relationship with the mother/parent, but on that of the social milieu. Several levels of containing can thus be distinguished: alongside the parent as container, there is the group, the whole of society, as an increasingly broadly understood container.

Aggression, attacks, and exclusion committed by groups of people against other groups of people can be particularly traumatic: at such times, those traumatized experience as a group that the milieu is indifferent, that it does not want to hear about the injury they have experienced, and in fact in extreme cases it supports the injury, and genocide. The partial or complete exclusion from a human community is an unprocessed trauma which follows and haunts later generations. It is traumatic not just for the victims and their descendants, but also for the perpetrators and their descendants, and even for the eye-witnesses, the passive observers of the event. Taboo memories that are swept out of the narrative are transmitted to children, though often in an unsymbolized form, which in more distant generations cannot be linked to the original trauma, or only very indirectly. The further we move from the trauma, the more difficult it is to identify the legacy. The original event is lost in the past, but its effect may be gathering strength. The memory of it is marked not by words, but by less symbolized contents: deep anxiety, psychosomatic symptoms, or even archaic, generalized feelings such as fear of strangers.

In addition to attempting to investigate the transgenerational effects of social traumas and possible therapies, the book deals particularly with the deep psychological effects of first-generation social-level traumas and with the risk factors that may lay the foundation for or mitigate the chances of the trauma being transmitted down the generations. In the framework of psychoanalytic theories, it deals with general psychological processes, which is to say it does not aim to analyze current affairs or processes in society. Through the psychological processes at the individual level it may, however, engender a better understanding of the psychological effects of processes in motion in society and the transgenerational traumatization being triggered today.

The first chapters of the book (chapters 1–3) investigate the direct and long-term impact of the traumatic event from the point of view of the first generation to suffer the trauma. We explore what psychological effects there might be from a serious trauma that the individual cannot process, in other words what the direct psychological impact of the trauma is, and what factors assist or impede the processing of the traumatic event and its integration into the individual's life history.

The second part of the book (chapters 4 and 5) deals with the new concepts we introduce, the transgenerational atmosphere, and the transgenerational self-experience. We define the concepts, and discuss the characteristics and functions of the transgenerational atmosphere.

The third and final section (chapters 6–8) focuses on the descendants. We examine how transgenerational trauma is transmitted, and what psychological effects and characteristics of relationships are typical of the following generations. We discuss special aspects of therapeutic work with the heirs of transgenerational trauma, then, drawing on the theoretical basis introduced by us and expounded in the previous sections, in the last chapter we suggest methodological changes that improve the efficacy of therapeutic work with the heirs of transgenerational trauma, and help us to understand the psychological processes operating within them.

By way of conclusion we asked renowned exponents of other fields (an anthropologist, a family therapist, a literary scholar, a historian, a memory researcher, a control systems specialist) each to write a brief reflection, freely associated with ideas raised in the book.

In addition to presenting the transgenerational psychological impacts of trauma, and the clinical work on it, the book puts forward a new theoretical framework for the understanding of transgenerational trauma. By introducing new concepts, we attempt to interpret from a new perspective the familiar psychological phenomena and observations from therapy already described by others. The scheme proposed here enables us to comprehend many familiar phenomena in a new theoretical framework, within which we can interpret areas such as: the psychological impact of the trauma on the first generation; the mode of transmission; the psychological impacts occurring in the heirs of the transgenerational trauma; and special therapeutic aspects. Building on this, the transgenerational atmosphere provides an opportunity for methodological considerations, for instance, the re-interpretation of phenomena previously interpreted as resistance, or negative therapeutic reaction, or for the introduction of changes in methodology that may improve the efficacy of work with transgenerational trauma.

The theoretical framework of the transgenerational atmosphere builds on many earlier well-established theories and observations: here we highlight only those we consider most decisive which have most shaped our approach. These are Sándor Ferenczi's theory of trauma; the findings of Hungarian Holocaust research, in particular the work of Teréz Virág; the phantom theory of Mária Török and Miklós Ábrahám, the "telescoping of generations" by Haydée Faimberg; Jeffrey Prager's social and anthropological approach emphasizing the role of the broader social context; and the self theory nature of the transmission of foreign events as described by Vamik D. Volkan.

In the formation of the theoretical concept of the transgenerational atmosphere, in addition to the influence of the dominant theories and literature, also important were the observations we gained during our therapeutic work with the heirs of transgenerational trauma. As well as our professional interest, like many other writers on this topic, our own family history and involvement motivated us to gain a better grasp of the psychological processes of transgenerational trauma, and this process of thinking and forming the theory together helped us to understand our own transgenerational legacy.

Our examples are fictitious stories based on true cases, derived from our own practice. All personal data (such as name, age, profession, or even sex or nationality) have been altered in order to protect the privacy of the individuals.

Introduction

During the development of the personality, individuals form an interior image of themselves (the self) through which the exterior and emotional events they are subject to, including traumatic events, can be experienced and interpreted. In healthy functioning, the self-narrative (the way individuals think of themselves) is continuous; there is a connection between the life events and feelings, and the life story can be narrated.

For both the development and the maintaining of a healthy personality, it is absolutely indispensable to have a sufficiently safe milieu, in the family and more broadly in society. A basic prerequisite for the formation of a coherent self is that there be good-enough early relations, which are able to mirror and contain the child's feelings and on which later relations can be built. However, for people to sustain self-coherence they need throughout their lives secure, functioning relationships, in which they see themselves mirrored.

At the same time every human being is dependent on the surrounding world, on society – the "good-enough" environment in the broad sense is a prerequisite for both the healthy development of personality and the maintenance of self-integration. Traumatic events that surpass the individual's ability to process them may for a shorter or longer time, or even permanently, break the individual's image of themselves: the event is, temporarily or permanently, impossible to integrate into the self-narrative. The subsequent psychological effect of the traumatic event depends on whether the individual is able, alone or with help, to restore the image of themselves, and find a place for the traumatic experience in the self-narrative. In this healing process the individual relies on inner resources (such as the inner core self that provides stability) and external resources (such as functioning relationships and a supportive social milieu).

Another important factor is the phase of the individual's development in which the traumatic event occurred. When undergoing development or when injured, the self is particularly vulnerable, since the individual's image of themselves is not continuous, and the self-narrative is fragmentary. Traumatic events occurring in this phase are particularly destructive, and self-coherence cannot be restored without help (for instance, in the case of child survivors of social traumas).

At the same time, there are some traumatic events that in the long term are able to break even the self-image of an individual with a well-formed stable self, and trust in the world (basic trust) is replaced by mistrust (the basic fault) (Balint, 1979, 1999). For instance, large-scale social traumas committed against humanity:

> During therapy with Holocaust survivors I have observed that social trauma can be understood as a special form of the Balint-style basic fault. This basic fault is however wider ranging than that used by Balint, the result of the mismatch between mother and child, and the non-equivalence between the individual and the outer world.
>
> (Virág, 1999, 283)

In this book we deal with the impact, the transmission, and the therapeutic approach to just such large social traumas caused by humankind.

Chapter 1

The impact of trauma

Healthy development of personality

During the healthy development of personality, the core self is formed as well as the fundamental structures that form identity (Stern, 1985, 2002; Pető, 2014, 51–69, 71–82). The core self ensures the sense of constancy, and through it the individual can perceive predictability. The core self is similar to the keel that steadies a yacht. If the individual gets into a storm (if they are affected by frustration, stress, crisis, or trauma) after a while, because of the "keel", they are able to right themselves to a stable state, integrating the experience, and perhaps even being enriched by it.

In addition to the security of the core self, the formation of other systems, those of self-experience and self-representation, is important, and through these the individual is able to react to changing circumstances (Kernberg, 2012). These reactions are also important elements of basic security, because they yield the experience that the individual is flexible, spontaneous, and creative. Through them the individual becomes capable of coping with unexpected, stressful, unpredictable situations, just like the yacht, where as well as the keel, the sails help it to respond. The two features interact, and their constant interaction is the basis of the development of the healthy personality.

For the formation and maintenance of a healthy personality, there must be a suitable milieu. The core self, the image the individual has of themselves, is born in a relationship: without a secure environment, one that is "good enough", with early relations able to hold and mirror, it cannot form (Winnicott, 1953, 1960). The empathetic response of the parent as a mirroring self-object is indispensable for the formation of the nuclear self. As the primary self-object, the parent handles the child as if it had a self – thus actually creating the basis for the healthy development of a self. Later, with the internalization of the mirroring function and the idealizing self-objects there may form what is known as a bipolar self, which now has its own ideal images and healthy ambitions, and is able to imagine the other as an independent being (Kohut, [1971], 2001; Fonagy and Target, 2005, 208–213). At the same time, although mirroring and idealized self-objects are internalized during early development of the self, an individual needs self-objects throughout his entire life in order to maintain self-cohesion, in other words to be able to imagine himself as a coherent whole.

During the development of the self, the child forms the ability to contain. Initially, the baby is not able to contain the unprocessed contents that flood it, and it needs another, the mother, or the caregiver, or to use one of Kohut's expressions, the mirroring self-object, for its containment function (Bion, 1959, 1962; Fonagy and Target, [2003], 2005, 157–161). The mother is able to contain the unsymbolized experiences of the baby, which it cannot do alone, to digest them, and to give them back in a digestible form and dosage (Ferro and Civitarese, 2016; Lőrincz et al., 2019). The baby will then be able to internalize these jointly processed contents, and will gradually acquire the ability to symbolize, to transform: as a result of the developmental process the individual will be able to give a name to his emotions, to interpret them, and to narrate them in the form of a coherent story. In parallel with this, the ability to mentalize also develops, in other words the individual becomes able to understand and contain not only his own mental states but those of others, and able to understand others' emotions and predict their actions (Allan et al., 2011). Building on all of this, there forms the security, or basic trust as Erikson terms it (1963), on which later relations can build, and which can be returned to after crisis or trauma.

The prerequisite for the development of the healthy self is thus the mother's ability to contain, to experience, and to make bearable the baby's unsymbolized feelings (known as beta elements). Insofar as the mother is not good enough at containing the baby's proto-emotional sensations, the capacity for symbolizing – the capability to think, the skill of forming and recreating a narrative, and the ability to mentalize may suffer (Ferro and Civitarese, 2016). Without a secure enough milieu, the individual's inner image of himself may become seriously fragmented and chaotic, and the individual may even become incapable of living, not only in the early phase of development, but at any time in their life. The ship (the personality) depends on the sea that bears it: on the one hand it must hold its course securely, remaining stable; on the other, it must be able to progress, being flexible. A well-constructed stable ship, with sufficient keel and sails, can withstand even a strong storm, but some storms are so destructive that they can severely damage or destroy even the most securely constructed ships. Such are the turbulent times, and unprocessed personal tragedies, that life may bring to the individual. The outcome depends largely on how the environment in the narrow and broader sense is able to help – in other words, the extent to which it is able to contain the traumatic, indigestible contents that swamp the individual. An environment capable of containment might operate in a similar way to the mother in the early relationship: it assists temporarily in containing and supporting the mental digestion process, then re-integrating into the self the unmetabolized psychic, physical, and affective experience.

Explosive phase

In the temporary explosive phase forming as the result of a shocking event, intensive processes are underway in the individual: experiences, emotions, moods, fears, thoughts, and memories occupy one and the same space. Nervous, hormonal, and physiological reactions are triggered. Conscious and unconscious visceral and nervous system processes, cognitive and emotional, somatic and mental processes interact with one another. This is when it is decided how the individual will move forward (Bakó, 2017, 220).

Possible effects of trauma

Whether or not the event proves to be traumatizing depends largely on

1. in which stage of personality development it affects the individual (whether the individual has the internal resources to protect and support themselves in processing the event);
2. what psychic state they are in at the time (can they mobilize the mental mechanisms for protection and processing);
3. how sensitive they are to the given problem, in other words, is it the kind of event the nature of which has previously been the cause of failure, or an event they would be able to process in a more balanced state;
4. whether they have an external relationship that can provide help;
5. what their relationship is to spirituality, transcendental matters, and religion. (Bakó, 2017, 220).

The shocking event and the traumatic reaction

Trauma is a reaction to a shocking event, when

1. the individual is not able to restore equilibrium with former resolution methods;
2. he/she experiences vulnerability as a result of the event;
3. under the threat of destruction, the self disintegrates, and thus is not able to coordinate protection in the resulting situation;
4. because of unbearable mental pain the disintegration becomes permanent;
5. memories become fractured, as memory removes the self from the shocking experiences;
6. the experience is not identified;
7. because of a change in the dimensions of time and space the individual feels lost;
8. the desire for self-destruction is present as a way of putting an end to the pressure. (Bakó, 2009, 21).

The word trauma is Greek in origin, and refers to a sudden, very powerful shock, causing physical or emotional injury or confusion (Tolcsvai Nagy, 2007, 1042).

As Ferenczi said, "In a traumatic situation the more-or-less whole world collapses, the defense mechanisms do not work, and we are left unprotected. So we are disappointed in ourselves." Ferenczi here describes the effect of trauma on the individual in *A trauma a pszichoanalízisben* (Trauma in psychoanalysis, Ferenczi, [1933], 2006b, 112). Shock is equivalent to the destruction of self-esteem and the ability to resist, from which flow the actions and thoughts that defend our own self (ibid.). The unexpected, sudden shock of a traumatic experience shakes the foundations of the individual's sense of security. The events penetrate into the deep structures of the personality and damage it (Lust, 1999, 72–87; Ajkay, 2016, 404–411). The traumatized individual feels that he or she is being destroyed, falling into a black hole (Hopper, 1991, 607–624). Kipper (1998, 113–121) writes that the trauma has the effect of changing biochemical, physical, perceptual, cognitive, emotional, behavioral, and psychological processes, which may result in failure in neurotransmitters, a rupture in connections between certain areas of the brain, and the switching off of sensorimotor memory. It thus simultaneously mobilizes primary thinking processes and distorted object relations, causing inadequate, intensive emotional reactions, primitive defense mechanisms, and uncontrolled behavior.

The person subject to the trauma undergoes a fundamental change, putting them in a state of chaos (Bakó, 2009). As a result of the trauma they lose their sense of security, of predictability. The trauma victim realizes that integrity is a mere illusion. The psychological space in which the traumatized individual lives and operates is characterized by constant elemental fear, weakness, and a lack of control over one's own fate (Hermann, 2003, 66–69). A contradictory presence takes shape in them, the simultaneous drive to remember and to forget, to uncover, understand, and confront the experience, and also to avoid it and ignore it (Bakó, 2005).

The traumatized person loses their ability to understand themselves. The cognitive and emotional functions become less effective and the role of control functions is reduced. The trauma victim is characterized by regressive operation, and symbolization – the ability to express important events verbally – is reduced. Thus, the individual loses the opportunity to narrate the traumatic event, and for its identifiability to aid the working-through process and self-healing.

Healthy processing of trauma

A shocking event does not cause trauma in every case; the self may be capable of dealing with it. The traumatized individual experiences the pain and suffering but is able to remain in contact with themselves, and the core self is not destroyed; in the process they go through after being overwhelmed they come to the surface. The experience permeates the entire personality, then gradually becomes a memory. The individual who experienced the traumatic event becomes able to integrate the experience, which becomes part of – but does not dominate – the personality. Whereas in pathological processing of trauma the individual has the sense that time stands still, and there is no integration.

Stages in the healthy processing of trauma

1. Experiencing the event. While experiencing the event, the traumatized individual remains in contact both with themselves, and with the reality of the external world. The inner core self does not disintegrate, thus the person, or the image they have of themselves, does not disappear. In the security of this constant presence they are able to bear the suffering, and they know they will survive. The basic trust in themselves remains constant. They become one with the experience, feeling the pain and suffering. They spend as much time in this state as they need.
2. Mourning. In the process of mourning, the traumatized person gradually relinquishes the actual person, but retains and internalizes the memory of and relationship with the person who died.
3. Integrating the experience. The previous two stages aid integration, which is the process in which the individual undergoes the experience or loss, and internalizes it.

In this respect, the experience of pain, suffering, and destruction is a healthy reaction to trauma. Through this the individual is able to experience the traumatic events and wrestle with them, to process and integrate them.

A 52-year-old woman who had lost her husband spoke of this inner process:

> I was extremely shaken by my husband's death. It was unexpected. I felt enormous pain, perhaps it annihilated me. I experienced the sense of being lost. I felt pain, but all the while I stayed in contact with myself. I wanted to experience the things I was feeling. I let go, losing myself in the experience, so that it would be with me. I didn't want to restrict myself, and took as much time as was necessary. The pain became a part of me. When the doctor suggested some tranquillizers, I refused. It was important to be with my children. I knew that the loss of their father was just as painful to them as to me. We supported each other. Then somehow – I don't know how because I thought things would stay like that for ever – after a year the pain lessened. Now I remember that time as one of the strongest emotional states of my life. It is important to me. It became part of me. It made me stronger, more complete.

In the healthy processing of the event a development can be observed: the experience with the traumatic event undergoes serious changes, and when it is internalized and integrated, it becomes a building block of the personality. Self-coherence is restored.

Pathological processing of the trauma

While in healthy processing of the trauma the individual experiences the traumatized emotional state, in pathological processing the experience becomes impossible to influence. As if it were not an inner entity that belonged to them, but some constant external risk, a nuclear charge in a capsule, which constantly irradiated the harmful substance (Rosenfeld, 1986, 56–57; Mészáros, 1990, 34). Because the individual cannot integrate the gravely traumatic experience, it seriously damages the self. The core self that provides security and continuity is damaged, and in the ensuing chaos the consolidating ability of the self is damaged, the self-narrative becomes fragmented, the individual is no longer able to react flexibly to events in the external world, and the body may become a carrier of experience, as one patient put it:

> I can't summon up my memories, but my body doesn't forget. There's a constant tension in me. As if I were living in constant fear. I've built a thick wall. At least that's what I thought, but it was like a dyke in summer. It collapsed over and over again. I always had to be on the alert, because there was the threat of flood. I'm overwhelmed by fear, it buries me, sweeps me away, erases me. This is the real trauma, which has no end. It's moved into my body. It keeps me in continual tension.

Because of damage to self-coherence, the disintegration of the self, this state of alert becomes constant (Cooper, 1986, 41–56). There is damage to the containing, identifying, integrating functions (e.g. perception, sensing, recognizing, thought, ascribing meaning), which would have the task of consolidating and relating the new events to earlier experiences, thus integrating them into the personality and the self-narrative. The self-structure may be damaged to the extent that the traumatized individual feels existence to be unbearable, and may react in one of the following, extremely pathological manners:

1. Self-destruction. The traumatized individual destroys himself, thus freeing himself from the traumatic experience.
2. Psychotic reaction. The individual cannot defend himself sufficiently, and becomes disintegrated: the experience crushes the individual's inner image of himself, and may lead to a psychotic state.
3. Splitting. The traumatized individual isolates himself from his emotions: he dissociates the painful feelings he feels will destroy him, thus achieving a sense of temporary relief. He simultaneously dissociates the reality of the external world, and retreats into an internal, intrasubjective reality.

Post-trauma intrasubjective experiencing and processing of the event

As a consequence of his dissociating internal and external contents, the traumatized individual is, psychologically speaking, left alone: he loses his relation both with external reality (he is unable to form relationships, or accept help) and with his own feelings. The intrasubjective reality grows in strength, and intersubjective effects weaken. Due to the intrasubjective living of the experience, the internal and external worlds are not differentiated. The post-trauma pathological experience is characterized by a permanent continuous readiness, a basic feeling of being under threat. Rather than objective time, the predominant time is the subjective, traumatic time. The experiences of the past are not able to become memories, they remain in the present, they define the traumatized individual's presence in the world, and also have an effect on the future. In this enclosed psychological space, the colored subjective experiencing prohibits relief in the individual, who is thus traumatized over and over.

The damaged self cannot shift the individual out of this state. The traumatized person is unable to reflect either on himself, or on the external world: he exists as if the sudden, unexpected event could repeat itself at any moment. He lives in this self-made intrasubjective space, and it is here that he operates his relations. It is through this space that he perceives, interprets, and reacts to the world and events around him. The following case is an example:

During therapy, Kamilla (whose stepfather regularly sexually abused her in childhood) discovered the "ready for anything" state that she experienced again and again in relationships with men. As she puts it: "With men, I feel that I have to protect myself. I'm like someone threatened by a great danger that could come any moment. My whole body is always tense. I never understood what caused it."

Kamilla told of several instances when after a sexual approach from a man she had become aggressive, defensive, and rushed off: "I almost always behave like a mad woman." In the ongoing therapy she is beginning to notice that it is as if she sees not her partner in his objective reality, but an experience from her own internal enclosed world, transposed onto the current relationship.

Chapter 2

From trauma to transgenerational trauma

The role of the containing function of society

As we saw in the early development of personality, it is basically the parent who reflects and contains the baby's feelings, interpreting and validating them. However, a person needs to receive mirroring not just in the early stages of development, but throughout his or her life. Individuals need not merely functioning relationships, but a milieu in a broader sense, in which they see themselves reflected, and which is able to contain them. The role of the social "mother-mirror" is among other things to reflect how the external world interprets what the individual has experienced, what for him is a traumatic experience.

In the case of social traumas, in terms of both the long-term psychological effect, and of the opportunities for healing, one crucial factor is that the same overwhelming unprocessable traumatic experience is shared by a whole community. If the trauma prompts sympathy and solidarity from the environment, if the environment is empathic, and reflects that this trauma is indeed a trauma, this aids the healing process. If, however, the social mirror is blind, insensitive, or if society itself is the perpetrator, then the traumatized individual or group is left alone with the experience. If the social processing of the trauma, the mourning process, fails to happen later too, there is a high chance the trauma will become transgenerational, and affect not only the victims, but the whole of society, for generations.

The reaction of the immediate and wider environment around the traumatized person is thus particularly important: if there is room for intersubjectivity – if there are still functional, reflective relationships, if the external world is empathic, if the trauma can be shared and narrated – the chance for correction is much greater. If, however, there is no suitable milieu – if the traumatic experience of a group cannot be shared at a social level – then the group-level experience of the trauma may worsen the individual's traumatization, and the trauma becomes uncontainable at the group level. The border between the life-world belonging to *me* and the one belonging to the *other* in the group sharing the experience becomes blurred: the *me* has the sense that the experience is generalized, and the *me*-experience thus becomes a group-level *we*-experience. A shared life-world may provide a kind of security, so those sharing trauma validate and conserve it, and are then more likely to transmit the experience.

Following the pattern of the early relationship, in the case of group-level traumatization, society – the environment in an even broader sense – may have a role to play in containing the unprocessed contents overwhelming a traumatized individual or group. A good enough milieu is able to help digest and render tolerable things that the traumatized individual or group alone cannot. Thus, the traumatic event can become integrated at both the personal and group levels. If, however, society as a whole is affected by and deeply involved in traumatization – involving almost every member of society as victim, perpetrator, or eye-witness – the entire society's capacity to contain and transform may be seriously compromised. A damaged society unable to symbolize – as when the mother's containing function is defective – is unable to operate as a container. It will not be able to temporarily contain the traumatized individual's undigested feelings, or help in the processing and re-integration of the experience. Dominance is given to more primitive functions working against integration – such as splitting, projection, and pathological projective identification. Without a container, the undigested experiences overwhelming the self find an archaic path for themselves, or are projected onto the external world.

The deepest level of transgenerational traumatization can be caused by social processes that affect the community of humans or a part of it, such as world wars, or a traumatizing generalized social process that affects many countries, or even continents. Such processes can be approached as damage to the container function of the whole of humanity: it is unable to contain and transform the archaic anxieties and destructive processes gathering strength in the individual and communities, anxieties, and processes that damage the self-integration not only of the individuals necessarily drawn into the process (blurring the boundary between the self and the other), but also destroy the already damaged container, the *we* in the very broad sense, thus questioning what it means to "be human". This degree of collapse of the container function can exert an effect on many coming generations.

Findings from Holocaust research

Our purpose in this summary is not to provide an overview of all the literature, but to highlight the typical features and observations regarding collective social traumas, on which we later build our own hypothesis. A large swathe of the literature is borne of Holocaust research, though the observations are not specific to the Holocaust, but can be found in the case of all collective traumas caused by humans, to humans.

The beginning of international Holocaust research, the end of the era of silence

The fundamental need of the traumatized individual, and the prerequisite for healing, is that the environment should not question what happened to him. Ferenczi's basic premise – that the traumatic event recounted by the patient took place – was an important realization, and brought a paradigm shift in trauma theory (Ferenczi, [1932], 1996, 1985, [1933], 2006b; Mészáros, 2003; Bakó and Zana, 2015). A similar change in theory was brought by the recognition of the role of silencing at the societal level in the case of the transgenerational impact of society-level traumas.

William G. Niederland was the first to describe the complex clinical syndrome observable in the survivors of concentration camps and other similarly serious, prolonged, and collective traumas, which he called survivor syndrome (Niederland, 1968, 313). The importance of the article was not merely the description of the syndrome, but that it broke the general silence surrounding the Holocaust, thereby opening the way for the processing of the trauma.

Following this, from the 1980s onwards, studies were published that discussed the impact of the trauma of the Holocaust on survivors and their children; the psychological impact of individual and collective silence (repression and denial); intergenerational communication and methods of transmission; and how this massive trauma is manifest in psychotherapeutic practice (Faimberg, 2005; Jucovy, 1985, 1992, 1994; Kestenberg, 1980, 1994).

Holocaust research in Hungary

Interest in the Holocaust in Hungary and the transgenerational effects on Hungarian Jews began in the early 1980s shortly after publication of the first international studies: this was the time when the first series of interviews were recorded in an organized and planned form, predominantly by psychologists and sociologists (Kovács, Lénárt, and Szász, 2014). On 9 November 1982 Teréz Virág gave a lecture at the Hungarian Academy of Sciences as part of a conference of the Hungarian Psychological Society, in which she recounted her experience of therapy with Holocaust survivors and their children (Virág, 1996, 5). This lecture meant the end of the era of silence: afterwards, research was begun in Hungary into the consequences of the Holocaust, and people began to speak about them. Several local and international projects were begun in Hungary (for instance, the Kestenberg project, which focused on child survivors), that aimed to examine the impact of the Holocaust on survivors and their children, such as the deep interview survey of Ferenc Erős, Kovács, and Lévai (1985), the case studies of Teréz Virág (1993, 1994, 1996), Judit Mészáros's case study (1990) (cit. in Vikár, 1994, 142), and the survey of Szilágyi et al. in 1986–87 (Cserne et al., [1990], 2014; Szilágyi et al., 1992; Kovács, Lénárt, and Szász, 2014; Pető, 2014, 213–227).

Society and trauma

The traumatic experience of the individual can only be understood completely with knowledge of the social environment around the individual (Virág, 1996, 5; Vikár, 1994, 142–143). In his study *Zsidó sors(ok) az analitikus rendelés tükrében* (Jewish destiny(ies) in the light of psychoanalytic practice), György Vikár made the important point that societal trauma and the destiny of the individual cannot be separated from one another: "In every case, the transmitted trauma of the Holocaust entered the context of the individual's personal development and life story, and it gained significance in this contextual system" (Vikár, 1994, 142). Transgenerational experiences, transmitted consciously or unconsciously, are linked in many ways to the life story of the individual (ibid., 143).

In her book *Emlékezés egy szederfára* (Memory of a mulberry tree) Teréz Virág emphasizes that the essence of the therapeutic approach is that "the child's problems cannot be understood independently of its parents and the circumstances in society" (Virág, 1996, 5). In the child's symptoms is reflected the terrible past, often unspoken, of the parents and grandparents.

This is particularly true in the case of collective traumas caused by people to people, the impact of which cannot be understood without a social and anthropological approach. Thus, in the case of societal trauma, not only the individual, but the whole of society is affected (Prager, 2003). The effect of the traumatic experience may be graver, particularly if the trauma has been rejected by the narrative of society and becomes a taboo: then it will be a collective traumatic experience for a whole generation. Because of the overwhelming nature of the collective trauma, the boundary between generations becomes blurred, and the next generation cannot build its own identity independently from its parents. The children of the traumatized generation, the second generation following the first, are called by Prager the "lost generation" (ibid.) These children, having lost their own childhood and identity, are predisposed to identify more with the traumatic past of their parents than with their own present (ibid., 174).

Risk factors for a trauma becoming transgenerational

Whether or not a trauma becomes transgenerational depends largely on the following closely connected risk factors:

1. Unshareability/Silence. Either the fact or the gravity of the trauma is questioned. The traumatized individual or group is left alone with the experience, which they cannot share with family members, friends, or the broader environment, and the trauma is silenced at the societal level too.
2. The absence of others sharing the same fate: the victim, or group of victims, is left alone. The victim has the experience that the closer and wider

environment does not feel what he feels (it lacks empathy), and its humanity becomes almost questionable.

3. Absence of a safe milieu. The processing of the trauma is possible only in a safe milieu, including the milieu in the closer sense (family, friends) and the broader milieu (society).

4. Absence of a narrative. The individual is able to integrate the experience (and thus to reintegrate the self) if the environment (family, society) is also capable of this. Thus, the event can be integrated into the life story and becomes narratable. If the experiences cannot be integrated they are split off, and the individual's image of themselves and consequently their self-narrative becomes fragmented.

5. Damage to the mourning process. Because of the splitting-off of the experience, in the absence of a continuous narrative the experience cannot become a memory, and the normal mourning process is damaged.

What can help in the healthy processing of trauma?

The trauma cannot "unhappen", it cannot be undone; we can only make the psychological space around the patient safe and acceptable (Bakó, 2017, 223). The purpose is for the traumatized person to be able to restore his own self-integrity, to integrate the event, and to order it into a coherent self-narrative. A prerequisite for this is acceptance and safety, not only in the broad social environment but also in the immediate family environment. However, silence at the societal level, turning the trauma into a taboo, and shame associated with the trauma, may at the societal level hamper the normal mourning process, and reinforce the difficulty of processing the trauma at the individual level, thus anticipating the trauma becoming transgenerational.

The role of witnesses and the sharing of the experience

During the processing of trauma, it is important for there to be a witness (Horváth, 2005, 7–15): someone who listens as the survivor narrates what has happened to him/her and who validates the experience, which thus is freed from the captivity of the intrasubjective space and becomes intersubjective, transformable, reality. The listening other, the witness, can be a therapist (Mészáros, 2003, 73), or a family member, a friend, or interviewer (Horváth and Zana, 2017, 84–90; Zana and Horváth, 2013, 234–235). In the intersubjective relationship the hitherto unshareable experience becomes a shareable, intersubjective experience (Ogden, 2004). By sharing the experience, the traumatized individual finds a partner in suffering, loss, unpredictability, isolation, and fear.

The role of witness can even be played by a work of art: in the narrative bearing witness, it expresses events in words, images, or music that bears witness, speaks a truth and the space of the text/image/music represents the intersubjective space, supposing an unknown but receptive other.

At the same time, it is important to note that this kind of witness role (the listening other, able to share and contain the experience) is essentially different from the role of eye witnesses to the traumatic experience, who in the majority of cases are also victims themselves. The eye-witnesses, often involved in the trauma as passive subjects, may also be traumatized and overwhelmed by their experiences: remembering may be traumatic for them too.

Pathological processing of transgenerational trauma

Sharing the traumatic intrasubjective experience: the creation of the transgenerational atmosphere

As we have seen, the unshareable experience is captive in the intrasubjective space. The traumatized individual feels they have no narrative that corresponds to the experience they have gone through. A traumatic experience that surpasses the individual's processing capacity is not integrated, and does not become a past memory; it remains present. The individual perceives, feels, relates, and acts in a manner solely defined by his internal world, rather than reacting to the external world. The events of the past are present not as memories, not *as-if* realities, but as reality itself.

A similar psychological space separated from the external world can be created as a result of any trauma. In the case of societal traumas, however, as we have mentioned, there is a qualitative difference: an entire generation shares the experience. If society is unable to integrate the experience, this community with the same experience validates the traumatic life-world for members of the group – in other words, the life-world of victimhood. This experience becomes a *we*-experience shared by a generation. The transgenerational atmosphere is thus distinguished from the traumatic life-world of the individual, by having not only a vertical aspect (affecting several generations of one family) but also a horizontal one: the *we*-experience spreads to the generation of the group who experienced the trauma.

In the interest of survival, the self gives up. Shrinking away and retreating from the external world and also from her own uncontainable feelings and experiences, she creates an intrapsychic reality. But this comes at a price. The feeling of trauma, of being threatened, becomes fixed or hibernates, and continues to exist as a psychic reality. The survivor perceives the current *here-and-now* through the filter of the trauma, and experiences even the present as threatening. The time frames of past, present, and future blur together. Thus, the survival defense mechanism itself becomes an obstacle, a pathology.

In the intrasubjective psychological space, robbed of some of his feelings and experiences, the traumatized individual is lonely, and feels that he cannot share what happened to him. To resolve this loneliness, to be able to take unspeakable feelings and share them with others, he chooses a more concrete form of sharing the experience. He is able to share the internal world he inhabits, the atmosphere he lives in, by creating an extended intrasubjective state or field of experience, through which he is able to relate to and communicate with others. This extended intrasubjective field can be called a "transgenerational atmosphere". This internal space – in which the trauma survivor lives out his important relationships – is safer for him than the threatening outside world. The survivor draws his environment, family – including yet to be born children – into this atmosphere, and it is mainly within and through the atmosphere that he is able to communicate and relate to them.

The transgenerational atmosphere created by the traumatized individual is thus an attempt to share the experience, to process the trauma and the mourning process, but in a more concrete, pathological form. Because there is an obstacle to intersubjective sharing, the traumatized individual extends the intrasubjective state, thus drawing his environment, the next generation, into what are predominantly undigested experiences. While in the case of a story transmitted verbally, as narrative memory, the witness (see the section *The role of witnesses and the sharing of the experience*) is able to stay at a safe distance from the traumatic experience, in the transgenerational trauma's expanded life-world this distance is lost, and the witness (in many cases the child of the victim) becomes part of the experience, a victim of both the original trauma and of the first-generation traumatized individual drawing them into the atmosphere. A crucial difference between the two ways of sharing the experience is that while in the case of narrative memory the traumatic event is transmitted in a digested, symbolized form, in the field of the atmosphere it is undigested feelings that are shared. While the symbolized memory exists in the past, the archaic memory through the atmosphere is temporally unstructured: past, present, and future are not demarcated; but rather are simultaneously existing realities.

Damage to the self and attempts at correction in transgenerational trauma

For the traumatized individual, the formation of the atmosphere can also be considered an adaptive defense mechanism: by shutting out and splitting from the reality of the external world, the individual creates an apparently safer internal psychic reality. However, in order to protect himself the survivor splits not only from external reality, but also from a part of his internal reality: his own uncontained feelings relating to the trauma. When the loss is unbearable and unprocessable, splitting off the trauma and the associated pain is a means of survival. However, by splitting from these emotions, there is also a split from a part of the personality, from parts of the self. From these traumatized parts of the self, there forms an inner deposit, isolated from other parts of the personality. This inner self-deposit, which almost perfectly corresponds to

Abraham and Toroks concept of the crypt (Abraham and Torok, 1984), stores both the traumatic experience and the feelings related to trauma and loss. These lockets within the personality, though isolated from it, store the traumatic experience and the undifferentiated, undigested memories of the traumatic experience: unintegrated, overly painful feelings, the memories of relationships with lost and unmourned family members. These complexes within the lockets may store not only the victim's own experiences, but other feelings and events, and even more concrete constructions such as images – for example the image of the aggressor (Volkan, 2013, 233).

The traumatic experience – the complex of feeling and event – can thus hibernate in the part of the self that stores it. The feelings stored in the split-off parts of the self, isolated from the external world, from the *here-and-now*, can no longer be accessed: they cannot be evoked, or dynamically transformed. They form an intrasubjective experience complex (a mass) in which feelings cannot be distinguished one from the other, or from the traumatic event itself. Since they are shut away, their intensity remains unchanged, they are untamed and unprocessed.

When the traumatized individual is affected by a trigger experience, it may evoke the original experience, which then bursts into consciousness. We have termed this experience a "flash experience": the flash experience is the undigested memory of the traumatic event, which as a consequence of the trigger experience overwhelms the self. The reaction and feeling in the given situation are not only disproportionately intense and destructive, but may also contain feelings such as shame, guilt, or aggression, which are impossible to understand in connection with the given event or the life history. These feelings, which may have been related to the original trauma, now as a result of being shut up and hibernated, adhere, undifferentiated, to other feelings.

In a trigger situation (which can be an external or internal event) the isolated part of the self is put into contact with the other parts of the self: they burst in, overwhelming the split-off part in a flash-like experience. Because that part is not an integral part of the self, and is not in a dynamic relationship to it, it is signed as alien, unacceptable, and the self quickly shuts itself out (in) again. The experience of being overwhelmed in a flash and the related emotions are often split off and considered not to have happened.

Though the traumatized individual protects himself from threatening contents, he also deprives himself of the possibility of correction. On one hand, by splitting off the reality of the *here-and-now*, of the external world, he filters out the opportunity for intersubjective relations; on the other hand, he also breaks the link with a part of his own inner reality: the feelings shut away in the damaged parts of the self are later not accessible to the self. Due to these pathological defense mechanisms, there may occur in the survivor a kind of emptiness or apathy: within his own self there are parts and feelings shut away that he is unable to connect to, as if these feelings did not exist or were lost to him.

The fragmented, vulnerable, traumatized self attempts correction, but because of the splitting of inner and outer contents, the self-correction mechanism is also damaged. The damaged self makes an attempt at correction by extending the borders of the self in such a way as to draw others into the individual's own intrasubjective space as part of the self. The transgenerational atmosphere as a psychological field gives psychological space that allows for the extension of borders of the self, the individual's own self: the survivor expands not only her own intersubjective life-world, but her self. There forms a divided self-state which we have termed the *we*-self. The survivor is able to relate to others, to share experiences and memories, and even to exist, only by making the partner, the child, a part of her self: she interprets them as a part of her own self. While a healthy mother-child relationship gives an opportunity for the child's self to be born as a separate self-state (the parent can imagine the child as an individual with an independent self), in the transgenerational atmosphere this is not possible: the parent's self is seriously damaged, "unviable" (in other words the damaged self is not able to function in an integrated manner, to contain difficult feelings, to form mature relationships). The *we*-self is thus inflexible, and does not allow the child's self to grow up, become independent, to separate. For the survivor, separation is incomprehensible, and equivalent to death. The child remains a part of the transgenerational *we*-self, as a supportive part of the parent's self.

Chapter 3

The first-generation impacts of collective societal traumas

The loss of basic trust

In order for a healthy personality to form and be maintained, a safe enough environment is indispensable, one which mirrors the individual in his own reality and uniqueness. In a retaining, predictable milieu the individual is able to feel safe, to form and maintain his identity, and to live his own life.

As a result of trauma, the individual's sense of safety in the world is deeply undermined, and the experience cannot be integrated. The traumatic experience becomes permanent, with the victim in a constant state of preparedness, unconsciously preparing for the trauma to be repeated at any moment. The experience is constantly present at the somatic level, influencing the processes of memory and perception. In this traumatized field of experience, the danger experienced in the past becomes timeless and infinite, and is projected onto the present day and the future, unable to become a memory. For traumatized individuals the vulnerable, damaged state threatens to become permanent and defines how they react to internal events (psychological) and external ones (in relationships and reality). Whether this state of preparedness remains constant, or is processed and integrated during the mourning process, depends largely on whether there are enduring relationships assisting the restoration of trust in the world.

In the case of societal traumas, the individual becomes particularly vulnerable, because he experiences uncertainty and defenselessness at the individual and the group levels. The state of basic trust is replaced by the state of rupture as in the mother-child relation, in the basic fault (Balint, 1979, 1999) and extended to the external world, in basic mistrust (Virág, 1999, 283). Approaching it differently, we could interpret basic trust as trust that the social environment, the human community, following the pattern of the early relationship, will be able to contain the contents overwhelming the individual or group. Basic mistrust can be linked to the collapse of the container function in the wider sense: the container function of the human community snaps, it is no longer able to contain the concrete, archaic-level destructive contents that threaten both the individual and the group, perhaps even with annihilation. (see *Introduction: The Role of the Containing Function of Society*)

Particularly vulnerable are the "children" of societal traumas, the child survivors. In an unsafe world even the good enough early relationships are damaged, because the mother's (or parent's) ability to contain and mirror is damaged. In order to contain, an individual needs inner safety, the knowledge that the problem, the bad feeling, will pass – and then the mother will be able to soothe the infant. This later becomes an internal modus operandi, with which the individual can later soothe him or herself. For children born at the time of large societal traumas, the default state is not basic trust but basic mistrust, and they then transmit this experience to their children in the subsequent generation, as has been observed in the case of the children of the Holocaust, the child survivors and their children (Kestenberg, 1980, 1994; Virág, 1999). The traumatized mother and the traumatized/traumatizing society mirror the child not in his own diversity and uniqueness, but as a member of a group, in uniformity with the group. For children born into this, the formation of their own identity is extremely difficult, an almost impossible task.

This phenomenon occurs not just in the survivors of wars and genocide, but in everyone whose trust in the world is damaged at the group level. This includes the trauma of any kind of exclusion or stigmatization. Basic mistrust belongs to the group and is transmitted to subsequent generations as a group experience: it defines the group's relationship to its environment, and prevents subsequent generations from relating as themselves to the world surrounding them. Thus, they often become victims or aggressors.

The deadened state

In order to survive, the traumatized individual gives himself up, and the parent, the survivor of the trauma, takes refuge from unprocessable external reality in a hibernated, almost "deadened" intrasubjective reality. This internal space, in which the individual tries to experience their important relationships, is safer for them than the external world: this "deadened" intrapsychic reality, shut off from the external world and certain internal contents, becomes to them reality. In this mode of psychic equivalence, the ability to distinguish between fantasy and reality collapses, and the individual experiences his internal world and ideas as an objective reality. He experiences any attempt to approach the *me* as a threat, and works intensively to defend himself. He distances himself from outer reality, filtering reality and disturbing information, thus trying to avoid another rupture. The traumatized person creates this intrasubjective reality in order to protect himself from the destructive threat which he ascribes to the outer world, but which is actually internal. Paradoxically, however, he preserves and stores it, maintaining the internal capsule that threatens him.

In the case of individual trauma, the environment mirrors back to the traumatized individual that this life-world, though reality for him, is not so for his environment, for everyone else. Thus, with time there is space for correction, at least for the child. But in the case of societal traumas, a whole community shares an overwhelming, unprocessed, traumatic experience. The individual senses that the experience is generalized, and the *me*-experience becomes a group-level *we*-experience. The boundary between the life-world of the *me* and the *other* becomes blurred; it blurs into the life-world of the other members of the traumatized generation. In the case of transgenerational traumas, the *we*-experience is reinforced by the distorted mirroring of the environment, thus validating and preserving this frozen (deadened) state. Those who shared the trauma validate the experience, and the shared life-world provides a kind of safety. If this is coupled with societal level silence or denial, this reinforces the living out of the group experiences as reality (the threat is experienced as constant, not only in the past) and the defense – the taking refuge in the intrasubjective reality, the "numb state" – is justified. The unreal world of the trauma thus becomes the *we*-experience of an entire social group, and considerably increases the chances that the traumatized generation will draw the subsequent generations into this atmosphere.

Traumatic space and time

The concept of time, like that of symbolized thinking, the naming of feelings, and the ability to mentalize, is an abstract construct created by humankind (Bion, 1962; Civitarese, 2019). Disturbances in the early relationship and the parent's inability to contain the emotions overwhelming the infant have an impact on all of a range of closely related processes: the development of symbolized thinking and the ability to mentalize, the process of remembering, the development of the concept of time, which interprets events in terms of past and present and preserves them as memories.

During early development the mother's inability to contain the infant's experience, or later a traumatic event, may lead to the collapse of the construct of space-time. In the absence of a container the infant, or later the traumatized adult, is unable to invest the undigested beta-elements with meaning, so is forced to project them into the external world – in other words, to evacuate them. This causes the collapse of the space-time construct.

In the case of transgenerational traumatization, due to the damage to the container functions at several levels, all these processes are damaged: as well as damage to the capacity for symbolization and mentalization, the space-time construct is also damaged, and in extreme cases the space-time construct collapses completely. In the traumatic intrasubjective field, the atmosphere, the experiences of the past are expanded to the present, and the victim experiences the risk, the threat, as if it were a current reality. Since the traumatic event and the related experience becomes concrete and timeless (at once unfinished and concluded), it is not able to become a memory. The traumatized individual thus falls into a distorted space-time trap, where the feeling of vulnerability becomes constant.

This intrasubjective experience determines his relationships with the external world, and to others.

The hibernated state with which the traumatized individual tries to defend herself, as we have seen, paradoxically preserves the experience of loss, making it permanent. It is the intrasubjective processes which are dominant; intersubjective events, those in the present, hold little sway. The traumatic experience is not processed, but freezes, and becomes a constant reference point. The survivor perceives the current *here-and-now* through the filter of the trauma, and experiences even the present as threatening. The flow of experience is not differentiated into time zones; past, present, and future merge together. Real, linear time is replaced by traumatic, circular, endless time. The traumatic moment is frozen, and it encapsulates the traumatic event too: the frozen, traumatic *happening* is not able to transform later into a *happened*, narratable, past event. The experience of continuity (life events follow one another and relate) is replaced by the experience of circularity (the same thing, always repeated). Meanwhile the experiences of the past repeatedly bursting into the consciousness can be understood as an attempt to symbolize and process the original, unintegrated traumatic experience.

In the case of transgenerational trauma, the self boundaries (the boundaries between the inner and outer psychological spaces, the self and the other) are damaged, both in the spatial (horizontal) and the temporal (longitudinal) dimensions. Since the trauma is experienced by society as a whole (as victim, perpetrator, or witness) the traumatic experience becomes a group experience, the boundary between the self and the other is blurred, and the traumatic *me*-experience becomes a *we*-experience at several levels. This is the cross-sectional or horizontal dimension of the damage to the self boundaries. If the traumatic event is not processed or integrated (for instance, due to silence in society) the *we*-experience becomes permanent. As this traumatized life-world, transgressing the boundaries of the self, becomes generalized and permanent, the transgenerational atmosphere is born, and the following generations are drawn into it. The damaged space-time field of the transgenerational atmosphere, which stores the frozen traumatic moment, creates an opportunity not only for the sharing of the traumatic life-world but also, as we have seen, the self-experience. The self boundaries are thus blurred in the following generations too, and this is now a longitudinal dimension of the damage to the self boundaries. The natural distance between generations disappears, the life-world of several generations overlaps and merges, and members of the following generation are unable to shape their own boundaries, their own identity (Faimberg, 2005; Prager, 2003; Mannheim, cited by, 2003, 175).

In transgenerational trauma the damage to space is inextricably linked to the damage to the temporal dimension; they build on one another and presume the existence of one another. Spatial damage, the blurring of self boundaries, creates an opening for the expansion of the traumatic time, within a generation and across generations: the perception of the trauma as frozen in time, timeless, makes it possible for *me*-experiences to blur together. Past, present, and future are not successive but simultaneously present realities, in which the life-worlds of generations do not succeed one another, but are simultaneously present.

The basic experience of the survivor generation, and especially that of the following generation, unable to break off from their parents, is a kind of spatial and temporal disorientation: it is impossible to know what is happening to whom, and when. Both the survivors, and the following generation sharing their life-world, experience something similar: the experience is not mine alone; it belongs to all, but at the same time no experience is solely mine. The external world loses its true colors and shapes "as if we saw everything through a curtain", as a third-generation Holocaust survivor put it.

Damage to the mourning process. The transgenerational secret, shame, and guilt

Already in the initial phase of Holocaust research, deep interviews with Holocaust survivors, their children, and grandchildren shed light on the role of the family secret, made more serious by the societal silence ("amnesia"), making it impossible for the trauma to become conscious and to be properly mourned (Kestenberg, 1980, 1994; Jucovy, 1985, 1992, 1994; Winship and Knowles, 1996, 259–261; Szilágyi et al., 1992, 120–123; Virág, 1993, 1994, 129–138; Cserne et al., 1989; Mészáros, 1990, 33; Pető, 1999; Erős, 2017). The "lack of mourning" weighs not only on the first generation suffering the trauma, but its impact can be noted over several generations. Indeed, some scholars point out that pathological mourning, or endless, unfinished mourning can cause an intensification of symptoms as it is transmitted across generations. They also highlight that in transmission, or in the background to the symptoms appearing in the third generation, in addition to family secrets and the silence and "no-go-areas" surrounding events, unconscious guilt is of crucial importance (Winship and Knowles, 1996, 260–264). Unconscious guilt and shame are key emotions that last for generations. They cannot be resolved, because their origin is shrouded in secrecy: what was the deed, or what should we be ashamed of?

One of the functions of the mourning process is for the traumatic experience, the loss, to be integrated into the self-narrative, and to become a memory. The lost family member becomes an internal object with whom dialogue continues, develops, and can be shaped even after loss of the person. It may give rise to many emotions, such as grief or anger. Insofar as the traumatic event is a secret, this inner dialogue is obstructed too, and the relationship can no longer be shaped dynamically – it is "deadened" (hibernated). Silence sends the message to the traumatized individual that the loss has not happened, or for some reason cannot be integrated, that "it's best to forget".

With no room for it in the narrative memory, the traumatic event (as we saw earlier) is split off from the other parts of the self, and is preserved as an inner capsule of the self. This inner "crypt" or capsule preserves the traumatic experience, as well as the unintegrated, unverbalized, undigested feelings related to the trauma and losses (such as shame, guilt, loss, anger, aggression) (Abraham and Torok, 1984; Rand, [1994], 2001, 64; Erős, 2017, 105–109). Without memory and the mourning process, these feelings cannot be distinguished from one another or from the event itself, and they recur unexpectedly with the same intensity for the traumatized individual and their descendants.

In the descendants, any trigger event, such as an actual loss or guilt, is capable of bringing up the original experience (a flash experience). The feeling is not only disproportionately intense and destructive, but is related to feelings, such as shame or guilt, that are incomprehensible in relation to the given event or personal life story.

The psychological effect of silence is thus most complex and far-reaching: it excludes the traumatic experience from the narrative, making it indigestible, unintegrateable, unmournable, while shut in the psychological capsule (the split-off part of the self) where emotions are undifferentiated. Shame or guilt may then "attach" inexplicably, in a generalized manner, in *here-and-now* situations to any relationship event in the traumatized individual and the following generations.

Memory Damage, narrative, and non-narrative forms of memory

The symbolized form of memory, the ability to narrate experiences in the form of a story, forms in parallel with the development of the ability to use language, to symbolize; in other words, narrative, narrative memory, is the result of the process of symbolization. Although in an intersubjective field this ability is congenital, symbolized thinking (the ability to give names to feelings and experiences, to interpret external and internal events, to place them in context with one another and in time, so they can be narrated) is the result of a developmental process. Infants need an "other" (a mother or caregiver) in order to develop the ability to think symbolically (Bion, 1962). Although the infant has the preconception of the relationship (the "breast") (Civitarese, 2019), early relationships play a crucial role in the development of this preconception into thought, then a thought network, a narrative that can be told, in which the feelings of the characters in the story can be understood, and their intentions identified. Similar to early relations, societal memory is only possible if the community, like the mother, is able to contain the indigestible traumatic contents and transform them into a coherent narrative.

In a healthy processing of trauma and mourning, memory makes it possible for the relationship with the lost other to remain even after the other's death, to develop dynamically, and finally become internal, a memory. If the trauma survivor cannot process the atrocities and losses experienced, the process of memory is seriously damaged, and memory will be fragmentary. Memories do not link continually one with the other, but isolated fragments of memory preserve the imprints of the sensory perceptions and affective states of the trauma. The split-off memory fragments are not integrated, and are not assimilated into a coherent self-narrative. In some cases, the damage can be such that there is no narrative component to the memory of the trauma: instead of explicit, verbal remembering there is only implicit, perceptual remembering. The memory of trauma is actually the sum of the unchanged, undigested sensory memory of the traumatic experience: a mass of images, sounds, smells, kinesthetic sensations, and intense, overwhelming waves of emotion. This very traumatic form of remembering is none other than the unchanged, undigested (unrepresented, unsymbolized) appearance of the feelings of the traumatic moment (Van Der Kolk and Fisler, 1996, 355–358).

If the process of remembering is seriously damaged, the survivor will not even be able to act as a credible witness, to give an account of what happened to him (Horváth, 2005, 7–15) (see also the section *The role of witnesses and the sharing of the experience*). The place of narrative is then taken by more concrete forms of remembering, as in the following excerpt from a case:

> One of the therapists in a psychotherapy institute was dealing with a woman of about 45 years old, a second-generation Holocaust survivor. Week after week the staff of the therapy institute heard the indescribable sobbing of the patient, and they experienced great suffering. In the institute's cafe they often shared their experiences with one another. The therapist was so deeply moved and burdened that after the sessions she needed to take a break to find her way back from this distraught state to herself. The painful sounds wafting out of the therapy session made the witnessing colleagues part of the atmosphere.

For the second and third generations, there is often no explanation for the parents' behavior, only the behavior itself, the parents' reaction to certain words or situations, as a model (Szilágyi et al., 1992, 121–124; Cserne et al., 1989; Mészáros, 1990, 33). The parent or grandparent does not speak of certain topics, and the child, apparently, cannot (Szilágyi et al., 1992, 121). Shut out from the narrative, traumatic experiences are transmitted via other channels, mostly unconsciously, for instance as a scene or as somatic sensations. In the example above, the overhearing of the sound of pain in a community therapy space recreated the helpless, frozen state of trauma. It mobilized a fear, pain, or loneliness that froze the entire therapy community, and made the therapist temporarily unable to work. The trauma appeared and was shared not as a memory, but as a present reality. At the same time this can be viewed as an unconscious attempt at processing: the experiences, which were unprocessable by the patient-therapist dyad, shifted into an expanded psychological space, where there was an opportunity to digest the event experienced. The patient's sobbing traumatized the people listening, but they were able to speak to each other about it.

Perhaps the most important form of symbolized remembering is narrative. The symbolization process itself means putting things into a narrative; the one remembering makes an attempt to place what has happened to him in the chronological order of life events. Additionally, narrative is a conscious or unconscious attempt to share, so there is an intersubjective aspect.

As the narrative forms, personality and narrative are in dynamic interaction with one another. The narrative mirrors the state of the person, but the very formation of the narrative helps to restore self-integrity. If an event or loss, even a very traumatic one, can be put into the self-narrative and recounted, that is already an important part of the healing process.

Damage to the process of mourning and remembering, however, is also reflected in a change in narrative. The narrative itself, and the narrative functions, may be damaged in trauma. The text carries the trauma on several levels, and the pain and damage can be heard in the text (Caruth, 1996, 2–4). The narrative may be damaged due to trauma, and the damaged, fragmentary narrative, trauma-narrative, can re-traumatize the traumatized individual by mirroring back to him/her the fragmented state of the self, the loss, and thus the narrative is unable to correct the fragmentation of the self (Horváth and Zana, 2017, 233). Although the traumatized individual attempts to speak of the events, the narrative collapses and the symbolization function is unable to operate. The trauma-narrative mirrors the trauma: events are not linked to one another, as if there were no connection between the events. In the trauma narrative time is not linear; it is circular, trauma time.

After trauma the continuity of the narrative may break, scars and hiatuses may appear in it, or certain words may become taboo (Virág, 1994, 137). This in itself is significant. Words may acquire a different meaning, or an altered connotation. Words or events that for others are neutral, may for the parents stir up disturbing memories, and the reactions to them transmit to the children the unknown, painful, shameful secret (Virág, 1996, 25). The narrative of an everyday neutral event (such as when the child sets out to the shops, to school, or on a trip) is invested with an unconscious surplus meaning (e.g. it is marked as dangerous). There is a mismatch between content of the text and its emotional meaning, so the narrative cannot be decoded by the child. Words, whose function was originally to mirror the internal and external worlds, no longer mirror the present, but instead the frozen reality of the trauma. For the traumatized individual words no longer have any weight, or meaning, while paradoxically every word has enormous weight. In fact, they often traumatize by no longer being able to fulfill their role: to mirror the internal world to the external, and vice versa.

Continuity

Post-trauma intrasubjective life-world is largely defined by the psychological impact of the traumatic event. The traumatized individual is confronted with the duality of continuity: the traumatic event, the life-world of the past, and the *here-and-now*, the life-world of the present, give continuity together, but mainly in a split manner, alternating with one another. If there is an opportunity for correction, the integration of the experience may begin, and the environment and the events of the present will be increasingly able to shape the life-world of the individual. Alongside the continuity of the trauma, the continuity of the present is given ever greater weight.

For survivors of serious societal traumas, if integration does not take place, the post-trauma intrasubjective life-world freezes and becomes permanent. The anxiety, fear, and pain originally linked to the trauma are present in the life of the survivor not as past emotions or memories, but as continually present psychic realities, preserving the experience of the trauma. However, this constant state of being under threat is unbearable, so the survivor hibernates, retreating from the threatening, undigestible internal psychic contents which he actually perceives as external. This deadened, traumatized life-world maintains continuity for him.

Meanwhile the survivor also has a relationship with the outside world, and is able to relate to the *here-and-now*. The continuity represented by the present reality does appear, albeit faintly. Relations in the present are necessary for him as confirmation that he is alive, even if he feels that a part of him has died or is lost. Yet these relationship experiences are weak, fragile, and unable to maintain continuity long-term. At the sign of any real or perceived threat, the survivor unconsciously retreats into the continuity of the traumatic life-world.

This duality of continuity sometimes overlaps, and sometimes alternates, but always belongs together. Simultaneously, these experiences create the link with the present and the past. For the traumatized individual living in the psychological space of this duality, it is important to maintain this duality, for this is what defines him, what makes him who he is.

Imagination

"The mother's adaption to the infant's needs, when good enough gives the infant the *illusion* that there is an external reality that corresponds to the infant's own capacity to create" (Winnicott, [1971], 1999, 12–13). In early development, if the illusion-disillusionment, satisfaction and frustration, is bearable and containable in the mother-child relationship, the area of illusion is given a shape, making way for what are known as the transitional object and transitional phenomena. The transitional object later helps separation, bridging the gap between me and not-me, between the internal and external realities (Winnicott, [1971], 1999, 12–13). The transitional object is then situated between the self and the external reality, in an intermediate space where symbols are created, where play and fantasy have their place throughout life (Fonagy and Target, [2003], 2005, 179).

The ability to fantasize, which is similar to the capacity for symbolic thinking, or the birth of the time-space construct, is an intersubjective formation born in a relationship able to contain the feelings of the infant; these abilities develop in parallel and interdependently. Fantasy, which develops simultaneously with the ability to symbolize, later moves along the plane of past-present-future. It can be detected independently in each domain of time, but also links them together, creating continuity between the time domains. This continuity is necessary for the linking up of reality and fantasy, but also for them to be differentiated. Imagination, which hovers around the border of the surreal, gives freedom, provides an area for play, and makes the individual creative. It is a transitional space where relationship situations can be played out, and fears and desires can be experienced. It is a safe, intersubjective experience lived out intrasubjectively. It helps prepare decisions, and makes it possible to imagine future situations.

However, for fantasy to operate healthily an environment able to contain is still needed: a transitional space in a broader sense is necessary. We can use fantasy healthily if we are aware that it is not identical with reality, but is merely an *as-if* reality. The role of fantasy is to separate extreme emotions from reality, and to handle symbols as symbols (Erős, 2017, 103).

In serious societal traumas, simultaneously with the container capacity of the environment, even the human community, the transitional space in the broad sense, collapses. The space for play with all abstract operations such as art, religion, abstract thinking, morality, etc., – things that make the external world comprehensible to the *me* – shrinks. The victims of a serious trauma that cannot be integrated have the experience that fantasy – fear, nightmares – may become real, that the ghostly becomes reality (Erős, 2017, 103). The boundary between *as-if* reality and reality is blurred, and giving free reign to the imagination is risky. The trauma as a surreal reality robs the individual of the *as-if* reality of fantasy. As the domains of time telescope together, the past fears experienced by the trauma victim are telescoped into the current present and become permanently valid. The experience of the past carries a constant danger for the individual. It is no longer the trauma itself that maintains traumatization, but the distorted imagination projected onto reality. This traumatic imagination is not free, not able to imagine more alternatives, so instead it projects the image of the trauma onto reality. An atmosphere is born which is sustained by a distorted imagination that permeates reality. In this way, the role of imagination as a healthy psychological phenomenon may even be eliminated.

Relationships

The trauma survivor tries to live out her important relationships in the intrasubjective space. In order to be able to relate to the other, she shares and expands this intrasubjective world, thus creating the transgenerational atmosphere. Predominantly unconsciously, she seeks out relationships which respect this modus operandi, where the relationships and the partners adapt to the atmosphere.

The birth of a child threatens this safely constructed internal reality, bringing in the external world, the other. This arouses a strong, unbearable anxiety in the parent. Thus, in order to protect the child and herself from the threatening external world (which is actually internal split-off contents), from its birth she draws the child into the atmosphere, and does not allow it to be born in its own right. Later every attempt by the child at separation, even the formation of its own self, is a serious threat for the parent, and cannot be allowed.

The child thus basically shares the intrasubjective world, the atmosphere, of the mother (the parent). The mother or parent looks on the child not as an individual with its own self, but as a part of herself: the child is actually a projected part of the mother's self. Thus, any attempt at separation is dangerous for her: the separation of the child would represent the loss of a part of the self, herself, which brings the threat of disintegration.

All this can be induced by a trauma unbearable for the individual. The role of the external world is at such times crucial, in terms of whether it mirrors back reality, or the false, distorted reality, whether it supports the maintenance of the traumatic life-world. In the case of serious societal traumas, a group shares the same experience, which validates the reality of the intrasubjective living-through of it (a sense of being threatened, for instance), and further reinforces the experience of the victim that it is safer to give up the self boundaries, and dissolve into the *we*-experience. For the trauma victim, an important step on which much depends is what partner he or she chooses: one with whom he/she shares the experience of traumatization, who matches the atmosphere, and thus reinforces it, or one who with time will be able to mirror the reality of *here-and-now* – which in the best of cases may be corrective, and may move the survivor from their own intrasubjective world.

Chapter 4

The transgenerational atmosphere

Characteristics of the transgenerational atmosphere

The instigators of the transgenerational atmosphere are the traumatized first generation, and the following generations are then drawn into the atmosphere, so the atmosphere is actually a shared intrasubjective field expanded to several generations. The sharing of the traumatized intrasubjective life-world through the atmosphere is thus an attempt to share the experience, but in a pathological, unsymbolized way. The transgenerational atmosphere is an unconscious way of preserving and transmitting the trauma and the related experiences and memories when there is no narrative remembering or intentional passing on of the experience. For the generations involved, the atmosphere is the space through which the trauma is lived out and transmitted, non-verbal remembering and non-verbal communication.

For the following generations the atmosphere is alien (yet somehow familiar), a sum of experiences and feelings that cannot be comprehended on the basis of their own life-story, or only with difficulty. It is a shared *we*-experience in which several generations are deeply involved, the life-worlds merge together and exist in a common field. The child and the following generation who are drawn into the atmosphere often experience the world as split, as two worlds existing in parallel: the frozen world of the past and the reality of the present exist as simultaneous realities.

A second-generation Holocaust survivor describes this state as follows:

> I read an article, I can't remember where, saying that when two cars or aircraft go too close to one another, the air current can tear the child out of the mother's arms. The air current is so strong that it's impossible to hold onto the child. Ever since I've been worried that this might happen, at any time, to anyone, even to me. It is unavoidable: however hard I cling onto my child, I can't protect him. I live in a state of constant anxiety and vulnerability.

This quotation offers an insight into the anxious life-world permeating the transgenerational atmosphere. The past, the experiences of the previous generation – that children can be snatched from the mother, who is helpless and vulnerable – is lived out as reality in the current day. Although the reality sense of the survivor was otherwise intact, often ordinary situations, conveyed in real or fake news, would trigger in her a serious, almost psychotic level of regression and anxiety. The feelings of helplessness and vulnerability are familiar to her, yet cannot be identified and are inconsistent with her present circumstances.

The functions of the transgenerational atmosphere

The atmosphere as a defense mechanism

The transgenerational atmosphere can be viewed as a defense mechanism, the damaged self's form of defense against disintegration. The unusual feature is that the atmosphere is not an individual's defense mechanism, but the quasi-psychotic defense mechanism of a group (a community and/or family).

One important element of the atmosphere as a defense mechanism is "splitting". However, by virtue of the giving up of the boundaries of the self, it has much in common with psychotic functioning.

When the loss is unbearable and cannot be processed, and forgetting – the splitting off of the trauma and the related pain and mourning – comes into play, then the projection of the unbearable contents is a means of survival. However, through splitting, it is not only painful feelings, but a part of the self, the personality, which is split off. Projecting it into the external world, into the other, he distances himself from parts of his own self.

In order to survive, the *me* gives itself up, as a whole. By loosening the boundaries of the self, he dissolves into the group sharing the experience, and flees into a shared *we*-experience. The boundaries of the self can be loosened not only between different generations of a traumatized family, but also between members of one generation or group who experienced a trauma. Thus, in the milieu of the atmosphere, the victim experiences not just his own trauma, but via the loosened boundaries of the self, he lives the trauma of others as if his own. Thus, the group experience becomes an individual experience too.

For the survivor the atmosphere is the milieu in which he can live safely; within it and through it alone can he relate to others. Consequently, the trauma survivor lives out his important relationships in this psychological space, drawing into it the as yet unborn child, who he is able to communicate with and relate to mainly in and through the atmosphere.

While through the "splitting off" of mourning he tries to rid himself of the painful feeling caused by past loss, he unwittingly uses the atmosphere to prevent losses projected into the future, by drawing the child into the atmosphere (the expanded intrasubjective space) and not allowing it to be born in its own right, with its own sovereign self. The child drawn into the atmosphere is a "part" of the parent; in other words, the child remains an auxiliary part of the self. Every attempt by the child at separation is dangerous and threatens the parent with the disintegration of the self, in that the parent may lose control over the part of his own self that he has projected into the child.

For the child born into the atmosphere this alternative reality is reality itself, since in the atmosphere created by the parent, the self-experience is shared. In the atmosphere the traumatic feeling of being threatened becomes fixed and continues to exist as a psychic reality. The child involved in the atmosphere experiences the current present as threatening, through the filter of the trauma. Meanwhile the atmosphere protects the child's self from disintegration. It keeps the undigested traumatic experiences, also inherited, at a distance, by displacing them from inside to outside, and projecting them into the external world. The child, who has no means of struggling with the traumatic self-experience encapsulated within his own self, like the parent experiences the external world as threatening, and as for the parent the world of the atmosphere represents safety to him.

From the age of 18, Zoltán made repeated attempts to separate from his mother, living with whom he often found unbearable. For instance, when he was 24 he decided to move to England for work:

> When I decided to go and work abroad, I did it because I couldn't stand living with my mother. I couldn't bear her selfishness, her tyranny. I wanted to flee from her. The important thing was not where I went, but to be away from her. I didn't yet have any experience of how I would live alone, without my mother. We were one together, so much that I couldn't even try [being myself].
>
> I went. I felt: wow, how brave I am, how great it will be. Don't imagine that's how it was. I couldn't fend for myself. All I could think of was what would be going on with my mother. I felt a very strong sense of guilt. While I was abroad, I hardly left my lodgings. I didn't even last a month. I came running home. Already on the day I came back, I really regretted it. Mother took possession of me again.
>
> My later attempts to become independent were no more successful. My mother didn't let me go, but I think *I* couldn't fend for myself either. I kept leaving, but I always ran back to her, to that painful togetherness.
>
> I thought it would be better after she died. It was worse.
>
> I got married, and ever since, I've been fighting with my wife.

Atmosphere as a form of retraumatization

Zoltán's mother returned from Auschwitz and died 20 years ago. At the age of 65, Zoltán still struggles with whether he has the right to be himself, to live in an independent relationship. After we have spent two years working to understand the self-traumatization repeated for decades, he describes his psychic state, as follows:

"I'm not guilty," says Zoltán, sitting up on the analyst's couch. "And it's not my fault she lived like the walking dead, that she was melancholy, constantly anxious, that she lived in fear. […] I wasn't allowed to live. The sense of guilt prevented me having my own life. She didn't let me go. It wasn't me. I didn't have a personality. […] I was in non-existence, in a terrible death, like my mother. […] I wanted to relate to others, but I worried something bad would happen to the person I approached, to whom I was attached, who was important to me."

The traumatic experience cannot be shared as it is, unsymbolized, and it remains buried in the atmosphere, unchanged in intensity and contents, then as undigested contents it is transmitted to the next generation, and because of the damage to the boundaries of the self, this content is marked as the heir's own. In the milieu of the atmosphere not only is the transgenerational self-experience, the *we*-experience, transmitted; but also, the transmission, the depositing, of the split part of the self that preserves the memory of the traumatic event takes place (Volkan, 2013). This "deposited" part of the self is mostly shut off and does not communicate with other parts of the self. However, it may give way to a trigger event, and then its impact is particularly traumatic and destructive: the heir is utterly defenseless against it, because he cannot relate the experience shut away in part of the self to his own experience, and thus cannot interpret or integrate it. In Zoltán's case, it was the relationship with his wife that brought to the surface his long incomprehensible, overwhelming sense of being threatened, that the other might die because of him.

Yet the subsequent generations are traumatized not only by inherited traumatic content, but by their own experience: the traumatized parent herself may become an aggressor, whether by identifying with the aggressor, or by placing the parts of the self that are unacceptable to themselves into the child (Kestenberg, 1980, 777, 796–797; Volkan, 2013, 233). In this way they experience the child as the aggressor, and the feelings transmitted by the child as threatening, hurtful. This is particularly traumatic for a member of the following generation, who sees himself mirrored in his mother's eyes sometimes as a loved/loveable being, often as a savior, and sometimes as an aggressor.

In the atmosphere created by the trauma victim, the heirs' range of action is restricted, which one of them described as follows:

I was only able to move within the framework my mother laid down for me. If I accepted it, I could even feel that I was free. She never listened to me, only in the situations when I strayed from this framework. If I kept to what she expected from me, for instance to obey her, to be always with her, not to have intentions of my own, to be her little boy, not to cause a problem, then she didn't hurt me.

She didn't love me. She didn't know how. She put up with me. On the other hand, for instance, if I wanted to be alone, she blackmailed me, and made me feel guilty.

She stunted me. She made life impossible for me. She destroyed me.

The atmosphere as a carrier of the experience and a form of sharing the experience

The transgenerational atmosphere is a form of remembering and of sharing the experience when there is no verbal remembering, and there are no memories, at least on the symbolized level. Those who have experienced severe trauma are able to share the unutterable memories buried in the psychic crypts (the hermetically sealed parts of the self, shut off from the other parts of the self) through the traumatized life-world, the transgenerational atmosphere.

The subsequent generations receive as their inheritance uncontainable, unsymbolized emotions, with this form of transmission of the experience replacing narrative. This traumatic experience is thus the history of the family. It is a memory of the people, of the world, that disappeared – disappeared but not without a trace.

This goes some way towards explaining why it is forbidden for the children to separate, to step outside the atmosphere. As long as the memories of the past (experiences, losses, feelings) are embedded in the gelatinous texture of the atmosphere, any attempt at separation is the same as total forgetting, which threatens the total disintegration of the self (both the individual and the *we*).

Drawn into the atmosphere the child becomes a victim, a witness drawn into the experience, a living memory, a "memorial candle" (see the section *Children not born for their own sake*). His unconscious mission is to preserve the unprocessed feelings and memories of the first generation. In this psychological space there is no room for the children's own experiences or memories, or at least only ones that suit the *we* life-world. In the shared atmosphere, the child partakes of the parent's inner reality, on which the external world, the current reality, has little bearing. Through the atmosphere the child enters the parents' life-world, though at the same time this life-world will be part of the child's own identity. The atmosphere influences the development of his personality from birth – indeed, right from the moment of conception. The heir is not able to shape a relationship to the external world, with others, in his own right; he perceives everything through the filter of the atmosphere, through the parental life-world. No sharp demarcation line can be drawn between the *me*-experience (or autonomous parts of the self) and the *we*-experience: even the *me*-experiences appear as part of the *we*-experience, and the *we*-experience is lived by the heir as *me*-experience.

Through the sharing of experience, the feeling and life-world of the child is not separate from the parent's. The child experiences loneliness, vulnerability, separation anxiety, as his own. He identifies with and remembers only the life-world of the atmosphere.

Anna is a third- and fourth-generation Holocaust survivor, whose grandmother and great-grandmother survived the concentration camp together. For Anna every separation situation entailed severe anxiety.

Every day I left my son Tamás in the kindergarten, or later when I let him go to school alone, over and over I felt I was seeing him for the last time. I often felt that every day we spent together might be the last. Although I know this isn't reality, the feeling is real and destructive.

For Anna's grandmother and great-grandmother, the possibility of their being separated and killed was reality. The fear and anxiety they experienced was proportionate to what happened to them. For Anna, although she knows that the fear and anxiety are disproportionate and unreal, this state – the transgenerational atmosphere – in the current situation is the only genuine psychic reality, her own psychic reality. Unrealistic, disproportionate fears in the current day become relevant and real in the intrasubjective space.

The atmosphere as a form of transmission of the trauma

Although the psychological characteristics of the transgenerational trauma are well covered in the literature, there are still many unresolved questions regarding the transmission process. In this section we try to investigate how transmission should be interpreted via the transgenerational atmosphere, how this special psychological field creates the possibility for the concrete/ unsymbolized traumatic feelings and experiences of previous generations to be passed on.

In this book we do not deal with biological/genetic/epigenetic transmission, though a thorough understanding of transmission undoubtedly entails these areas too. In recent years a growing body of research has dealt with the epigenetic impact of severe trauma and its transmission – specifically through those epigenetic changes which are responsible for the genetic regulation of the hypothalamus-pituitary-adrenal axis. The transmission of epigenetic alterations may explain the long-term transgenerational impact of acute stress, and PTSD (post-traumatic stress disorder) (Baradon, 2010; Perroud et al., 2014; Ramo-Fernández et al., 2015; Yehuda et al., 2016; Felsen, 2017; Youssef et al., 2018).

When trauma is experienced, the biological-hormonal reactions are still adaptive and may react to extreme environmental conditions. However, in the subsequent generations the transmission becomes maladaptive, because the stress-reaction is no longer to the given environment, but to an earlier, extremely stressful situation. It would be interesting, but beyond the scope of this book, to compare the findings of psychological and genetic research, such as the expansion of the self or the transposition of a part of the self, and the mechanism of epigenetic transmission.

In the case of extreme societal traumas, we are dealing not with inheritance in the traditional sense – not an inheritance that can be identified with, rebelled against, and which, through the dynamic of identification and rebellion can be integrated. In the case of transgenerational involvement several generations share the same life-world, as if newer generations were not capable of rebellion, of change, or of creating a frame of reference different to that of their parents. The natural distance between the generations disappears, and generations lose their own identity. The life-world and history of several generations may telescope (Prager, 2003; Mannheim, cited by, 2003, 175; Faimberg, 2005, 8–9). As a result of this telescoping of generations (Faimberg, 2005, 4–18), the subsequent generations are born and brought up in the threatening, damaged state of risk and *me*-loss of their parents' world.

The literature on transgenerational trauma has since its inception tried to comprehend the process by which traumatic experiences are transmitted from generation to generation. Szondi ([1937], 1992, 1996, 69–72) used the term "family unconscious" to account for the emergence of archaic endeavors, patterns, and motifs in the destiny of the descendants. In the light of recent research, particularly interesting and relevant is Szondi's hypothesis regarding the genetic (biological) transmission of these phenomena.

Holocaust research revealed another development in this area. Not only was the role of repression – particularly at the societal level – recognized early on as a factor in causing symptoms, but so was the role of denial in transmitting trauma between generations, bringing the past into the present (Jucovy, 1985, 1992, 1994; Kestenberg, 1980, 1994; Faimberg, 2005).

Ábrahám and Török (Abraham and Torok, 1984) use the words "crypt" and "phantom" to describe the nonverbal transmission of family secrets. While the "crypt" signifies a psychic construct that derives from the individual's own life history, the "phantom" is an alien body, the unwitting transmission of somebody else's secrets and the associated unconscious feelings to the following generations. The hypothesis of these authors is revolutionary in the way it postulates the appearance of an alien part – the phantom – in the heirs, an experience from the previous generation, which cannot be explained in terms of the individual's life experience (ibid., 222–225). Ábrahám describes the transmission process as follows:

> ... the phantom is a construct of the unconscious which was never conscious, and there was good reason for this. It moves from the parent's unconscious, in a manner yet to be determined, to that of the child. The function of the phantom obviously differs from that of dynamic repression. The phantom [...] operates like a ventriloquist, like an alien within the subject's own mental topography.
>
> (Ábrahám, [1975, 1987], 2001, 68).

> The "phantom" is a radically new trend in Freudian and post-Freudian psychopathological theories: from here on symptoms can be traced back not just to the personal life-experiences of the individual, but to someone else's psychological conflicts, traumas, and secrets.
>
> (Rand, [1994], 2001, 63).

Volkan (2013) offers an interesting self-theory explanation for the transmission of alien experiences. Volkan calls the phenomenon a "deposit representation". The parent deposits, or projects, a damaged "self-image" into the child. These self-images absorb traumatic experiences and events, but in a manner undifferentiated: the image may be that of the victim, the perpetrator, or the aggressor. The purpose of the deposit is for the traumatized parent to rid themselves of the unbearably painful image – in fact a part of the parent's self. The process differs essentially from that of identification, in which the child is an active participant, filtering through his own personality the images and feelings transmitted by the parent. In the case of the deposit, the child plays a passive role in the process. The parent, the adult, aggressively influences the child's personality development with the insertion of alien images. In other words, the adult uses the child (albeit mainly unconsciously) to store his own and other self-images (ibid., 233). This form of transmission described by Volkan is almost totally unsymbolized, and the heirs have no chance of decoding the experiences.

The transgenerational trauma theory we put forward here builds largely on the hypotheses cited, but the cited hypotheses can be understood within the theoretical framework of the atmosphere.

The significance of the transgenerational atmosphere lies in how it helps us to better understand how the life-world of the parents is shared and the split parts of the self are transmitted to subsequent generations. The expanded intra-subjective field of the transgenerational atmosphere provides an opportunity for the expansion of the parental self, thus the boundary between the parent's self and the child's is blurred, and there forms a shared *we*-self, with a shared *we*-experience. The psychological space of the atmosphere also makes it possible for isolated, split-off parts within the parent's self to be transmitted directly.

Török and Ábrahám's concept of the "crypt" in many respects matches our thinking about the first-generation impact of the trauma. Under the impact of the unprocessed and unshareable trauma, a part of the self – which contains the traumatic event itself, the undigested feelings and experiences – splits away. This hibernating, dormant part of the self, or crypt, does not communicate with other parts of the self, and preserves the unprocessed trauma. This corresponds to the damaged self-images in Volkan's theory, which the parent cannot contain. It can also be postulated that these self-fragments store the undigested, unchanged preserved sensation of the moment of trauma: not only images, but smells, sounds, and physical sensations (Van Der Kolk and Fisler, 1996, 355–358). Although the split part of the self and the associated experience are cut off from the narrative, from remembering and from all more symbolized forms of transmission, they are given to subsequent generations, for whom they appear mostly as alien elements – a phantom, or a deposit representation. The child receives the "phantom" experience not in a processed form, but as an undigested self-experience (a hibernated part of the self), as a visceral non-mentalized memory of the trauma. But for the heir, the inherited, split element (deposit) is only partially alien, since in the shared psychological space, it becomes his own. It is harmful, because it is present mainly as an absence (as sealed content) but it is particularly damaging and traumatic when released (in a flash experience) and overwhelms the heir with undigested, alien feelings (as for example, acute anxiety, terror, emptiness, sadness, depression etc).

It is in the family's interest to maintain the transgenerational atmosphere. The interest for the first generation, for those who were actually traumatized, is that it draws the subsequent generations into a shared experience, so they are not left alone, and the experience of loneliness thus becomes shareable and thus more tolerable. Here the parent uses the child: not only to contain undigested feelings and parts of the self (Volkan, 2013), but also as a part of the parent's own self. Without the child, as a part of the self, the parent cannot survive, at least so (s)he feels. The child has a similar experience: because his self is integrally connected to the parent's, their life-world and feeling-world are not demarcated, and separation threatens his/her existence, or self-integration.

The transgenerational atmosphere may also come about in the case of family traumas, when what has happened is for some reason unspeakable (for instance, shame is associated with the trauma, such as in the case of murder or sexual abuse). A lighter atmosphere enveloping one family has a greater chance of lessening from generation to generation; the transmission effect weakens, because as the trauma recedes in time, the external world prevails in its role of controlling, mirroring reality, and containing.

However, the impact of the atmosphere formed in societal traumas does not lessen, indeed it can gather strength from one generation to the next. The broader environment plays a role in sustaining it and its long-term destructive influence, when it is unable to contain the trauma, and either fails to mirror or is distorting in its mirroring: partly by denying the trauma, and partly by offering a community of shared experience (for instance a shared victim role). If the social environment reinforces the unreal world of the atmosphere through silence or marginalization then the life-world of the atmosphere is confirmed, validated, and the transmission process may affect many generations to come.

The meeting of transgenerational atmospheres

For large societal traumas the whole of society is involved and traumatized, participating in the trauma either as victims, as perpetrators, or as eyewitnesses. The more the jointly experienced trauma is shut out from narrative memory, the more primitive, non-narrative forms of remembering gain ground. Each group creates its own *we*-experience and so expanded psychological spaces, atmospheres take shape, which on the one hand preserve the undigested memory of the trauma unchanged and shut away, and on the other hand provide a milieu for the non-symbolic transmission of the experience within the group (transversely) and between generations (longitudinally). The transgenerational atmospheres of various social groups can exist in parallel over several generations, without communicating with one another.

One example of this is Hungarian society. From the Second World War to the current day, there has been no processing, encompassing the whole of society, of the trauma of either the Holocaust or the communist regime; there has been no dialogue that would have been able to draw in all the groups affected in these successive, integrally related traumas (Bakó and Zana, 2017).

The annihilation of the Jewish community in Hungary began relatively late, but was conducted extremely quickly and efficiently. This manner of implementation is a particularly burdensome legacy for the descendants of the victims and survivors, but also even for the descendants of the perpetrators (Horváth, 2005, 7–8). This legacy, never resolved at societal level, has haunted Hungarian society ever since.

After the Second World War, the Holocaust played a central role in the lives of Jewish survivors and their descendants in the shaping of their identity. For Jews in Hungary, who felt Hungarian and had assimilated well before the war, it was a particularly deep trauma that society excluded them and deprived them of their Hungarian identity. This identity crisis was nuanced and made more complex by the socialist-communist dictatorship in power from 1948 to 1989, then by the change of regime at the end of the 1980s. Vikár (1994) uses the expression "double sandbag" to illustrate the post-Holocaust identity crisis:

> However, the generation of Hungarian Jews who grew up after the war often carry a second sandbag on their shoulders. Some of their parents returning home after exile from persecution […] enthusiastically joined the new system, which promised them freedom, equal rights, and opened the way to self-realization. Some came into positions of power. When the violations of the law were revealed, the structural inadequacy and economic flaws of the socialist system became apparent, and the second generation had to wrestle with another ignominy: their parents had supported an oppressive regime.
>
> (Vikár, 1994, 143).

The faith they placed in the communist system helped many survivors and their descendants grapple with the shocking effects of the Holocaust, but the change of regime and the concomitant disappointment, sense of shame, and the flaring up of anti-Semitism following the change resulted in an identity crisis for the entire Hungarian Jewish community, in many cases calling forth the long "silent" original trauma, the Holocaust.

Much less is said about what a complex legacy, what a "double sandbag" the non-Jewish population shoulders. While research into the transgenerational impact of the Holocaust on the Jewish community began in the 1980s, no such surveys were made concerning the non-Jewish Hungarian population, so we can only make broad deductions of the more general psychological processes. In the Second World War there were perpetrators whose descendants live with this traumatic legacy. There were eye-witnesses who may have been present in many ways, as aggressors, as victims, or as a combination of the two. Due to the passivity of the role, the witness can also be considered a victim, which for the descendants can become a particularly complicated legacy. Although since the 1980s much has been said, written, and researched regarding the Holocaust and the psychological damage characteristic of Holocaust survivors and their descendants, in Hungary (unlike Germany for instance) there has still been no processing at the societal level; indeed, with the change of regime more unspoken tensions have arisen. There has been no social inquiry into the role of the Hungarian population in the deportation of the Jews (this has largely been blamed on the Germans), nor has there been any society-level forum regarding the role of the Jews who survived the Holocaust and their descendants in the socialist-communist regime. Thus, between the Jewish (pre-dominantly assimilated, but ambivalent in identity) and non-Jewish Hungarian population there is a largely unspoken and largely unconscious chasm, unbridgeable because it is unseen. This "story" has not been transmitted verbally due to the taboos and silence, so it has been "transmitted" non-verbally, thus hampering dialogue and the resolution of tensions.

The original, unprocessed traumas, the life-world of the trauma, is preserved in a hibernated dormant state, like a time-bomb, and due to a trigger experience (such as a current social-economic crisis, a migration crisis) it may rise to the surface and be activated. The undigested contents hitherto sealed in the capsule (fear, anger, helplessness, etc.) seek and find an object for themselves in the *here-and-now*. The disproportionate emotions released from within are projected onto other social or ethnic groups in an attempt to destroy the source of fear in the present. On the basis of the *we*-experience, the *me* reacts disproportionately intensely to the events of the present: it becomes an aggressor, an excluder, or may even experience a sense of persecution, of being threatened. The individual reacts not to the interpersonal events of the *here-and-now* but to the group experience, finding security in the *we*-experience. The meeting is not of individuals, but of *we*-experiences, which no longer react to the current event or to each other, but to an event and relationships in the past.

With a lack of genuine dialogue, transgenerational atmospheres can remain in parallel for decades, or even centuries. The groups' perception of one another is over-simplified, on the basis of the persecutor/persecuted dynamic, and the projections and projective identifications may haunt society for many, many years. If, however, they can meet in reality, and listen to and understand one another, the events and injuries of the present can with time separate from the injuries of the past projected onto the present, giving room for a more realistic relationship.

Chapter 5

The transgenerational self-experience

The we-self

In a healthy parent-child relationship the parent is present in the child's life as a self-object. She is a model, a point of reference, a safe milieu, the primary satisfier of needs also in the psychological sense. Through her the child is able to create his own core self, which like a keel on a yacht, provides internal stability, and thus he is able to change and adapt dynamically to the external world. The parent allows and indeed assists and encourages the child in this change, and in the formation of his own personality.

This process takes place in an experiential milieu created jointly by the parent and child, while each possesses his/her own internal psychological space, separated from the other. A healthy union takes shape, a healthy mother-child we-experience, which is capable of changing flexibly, of following the developmental needs of the child. In the jointly created experiential field they interact with one another, through which both of their personalities develop. This shared experience makes it possible for the child to develop a stable, independent self (me-identity), and for the self to be integrated. A good enough early relationship and healthy development of the self creates room for the operation of normal projective identification mechanisms, which later serve as the basis for empathy and understanding (Bion, 1962; Fonagy and Target, 2005, 158).

In a family with transgenerational trauma the development of the child's self and the parent's self happens very differently. The survivor, who alone is not able to resolve the feeling of "a deadened state" and reintegrate his own split parts of the self, will try to rely on external self-parts. The birth of a child assists in this: the parent interprets the child not as an independent other, but rather as a part of her own self. The space-time field typical of the atmosphere provides a suitable milieu for the expansions of the parental self, for the creation of the transgenerational we-self. This atmosphere, as a damaged psychological space, is not able to contain or transform either the mother's or the child's undigested sensations into something digestible, so it is not able to operate as a healthy container. Rather than more mature psychological mechanisms, the dominant mechanisms are pathological, such as projection, pathological projective identification, and splitting. Not only is the mother unable to contain the undigested sensations of the infant, but she tries to use him as an auxiliary part of the self, to contain her own undigested sensations, projecting into the child the split, pathological inner contents. This mechanism prevents the development of the normal regulation of feeling, the self-soothing ability: like the mother, the child will be compelled to evacuate the contents that overwhelm him into the external world, into an other, or into a sealed internal space.

The development of the self of the following generation is basically defined by the experiences had in the transgenerational atmosphere, the parent's expanded intrasubjective space – and not by actual reality. The heir, the child, is born into a community sharing an experience, which transmits a sense of being threatened and persecuted. For him, the world is as he experiences it through the traumatized/traumatizing parent. He perceives the world surrounding him not as it truly happens, but through the atmosphere created by the parent. The original trauma, at which he was not present, he now experiences through the behavior and reactions of the parent: for him, the danger is a constantly present state.

The parent experiences the birth of the child as an intrasubjective process, rather than intersubjective. When the child is born, the parent does not meet it, or mirror it. What is created is not an intersubjective self-other relationship, but an expanded self-state. The child has a mission: to make the "deadened" parent alive again, to "give meaning" to her life: the child as a part of the parent's self may represent experiences and feelings such as happiness, hope, or success. Children not born for their own sake – who see reflected in their mother's eyes something other than themselves – with a lack of intersubjective relatedness, are not able to build their own core self and integrated self, or to feel security, and their own self and the parental self do not separate from one another.

The parent sees and experiences and comes into contact not with the child, but finds a space for it in her own intrasubjective world, in the trap of the trauma – as a part of her own self. Thus, the child has no chance of perceiving the world but through the expanded, distorted, intrasubjective community sharing the experience. At the same time, in the shared experiential field, the child is not simply subjected to the experience: its experience of the event may affect the parent in return, through which it reinforces the parent's distorted experience of the event. Thus, the parent and the child keep each other in the atmosphere, in the identity given by the *we*-self.

Every attempt at separation is mortally threatening to both the parent and the child. For the parent, the risk is that with the separation of the child she will lose a part of her own self, moreover the very part of herself that keeps her alive. The child experiences that it kills the mother – not in a symbolic, but a real sense, so the thought of separation brings unbearable guilt. After all, leaving the relationship would endanger not only the mother, but the child too. Without the *we*, which represents to him continuity and security, self-integrity – he feels unable to live. If the child wanted to separate, he would lose the *we*-self that functions as a core self. The *we*-identity simultaneously provides a familiar, secure experience, while due to the permeability of the self boundaries, the fears and sense of being threatened flow from the trau-matized victim to the heir.

The development of the self proceeds on two paths. In parallel with the injury, genuine attachment may form based on present relationships, and with good-enough early relationships there may be satisfactory interpersonal devel-opment, as a result of which mature, well-operating parts of the self (may) come into being. The joint presence of the relatively mature parts of the self and the *we*-self creates an unusual pattern; without a unified sense of self, an integrated self, and with the continuous presence of the *we*-self, the relatively well-functioning parts of the self are highly vulnerable to damage. They cannot react freely to the reality of the *here-and-now*, that is, they cannot relate dynamically to the other in the present.

The self-part enclosed in the capsule in the following generation

As we saw in Chapter 1, under the impact of the unprocessed and unshare-able trauma, a part of the self – which contains the traumatic event itself, and the undigested feelings and experiences – splits away. This hibernated part of the self does not communicate with other parts of the self, and pre-serves the unprocessed trauma.

The expanded intrasubjective field created by the trauma victim, the transge-nerational atmosphere, also makes it possible for these split parts of the self to be shared directly with the next generation, bypassing the process of symbol-ization (see the section *The atmosphere as a form of transmission of trauma*). These deposits (Volkan, 2013) are alien parts of the self, which contain undi-gestible contents (images, experiences, sensations, and events). Because the child's self is involved in the *we*-self, these parts of the self, although alien, become parts of his own self.

When this shut-off part of the self, which has been taken in an undigested form, and the experiences (images) enclosed in it bursts through, it is particularly threatening and incomprehensible for the child. Because he has no relationship to it in his own right, he perceives it not as a part of his own inner self, but as a threatening external attack, locat-ing the feeling in his narrower or broader environment. In this state of being under threat, the familiar world of the atmosphere provides security – at least, this is the experience of the heir. Like the parent, he finds refuge in the hibernated *we*-state, which keeps the perceived threat of the external world at a distance.

The heir is defenseless against the parent. The atmosphere, which he has so often experienced as a protection, can become a severely traumatizing milieu. The child is the guarantee of the parent's "happiness": not a separate person, but an auxiliary part of the self, whose function is to keep the parent "alive". Incorporated into the atmosphere, the child feels loved and accepted. The parent, however, who is occasionally overwhelmed by the traumatic contents (in a flash experience), tries to locate them outside herself, to project them: into the external world, or into the child who functions as a part of her own self, ascribing to him/her the unbearably difficult feelings. As we have seen, in these deposits are undigested events, images, and sensations; even the image of the aggressor may be preserved (Volkan, 2013). Thus, the parent might possibly perceive the child as the aggressor in these periods, which periods later are often split off, forgotten by the parent. This reaction, these feelings, are unprocessable, incomprehensible to the child who experiences constant guilt, though he or she does not understand what he or she has done wrong.

In transgenerational trauma, where the traumatic experience is shared by an entire generation, the self boundaries may blur not only longitudinally, through several generations of a family, but also transversely, within the affected group. The traumatic experiential field of the transgenerational atmosphere expands to the entire group: this is not the expansion of the intrasubjective life-world of one traumatized person, but the expansion of a traumatic group experience. In this way, the *we*-experience is shared not only by several generations of one family, but several generations of the traumatized group. In this expanded field we cannot rule out a transmission mechanism on the part of the self, when an alien experience-complex, a deposit containing the traumatic experience appears in the family *we*-experience – which although originally alien, still becomes a part of the self. In subsequent generations it is impossible to identify not only whose experience it was at the family level in the previous generation, but even whose experience it was at the group level. In the inherited life-world or self-experience, the group-level *we*-experience, the family *we*-experience, and the *me*-experience based on one's own life events are almost indivisibly intertwined.

The atmosphere as a primitive defense mechanism in the next generation

As we saw earlier, for the one who experienced the trauma, the splitting off of the painful feelings (and with them a part of the self) and the formation of the atmosphere can be considered a defense mechanism. This is the atmosphere the child is born into. For him, the atmosphere is both a traumatic milieu and a defense. Without a stable core self of his own, he needs the parental self that keeps him alive and the associated self-experiences. It is in his interest to maintain the atmosphere as a primitive self-defense mechanism.

Like the parent, the heir involved in the atmosphere perceives the external world as threatening persecution but paradoxically he also perceives that the atmosphere provides protection. The defense function of the atmosphere lies in that it keeps split off the parts of the self that contain internal threatening contents. The heir is indeed helpless against these contents, which for him are largely alien, and has no chance of integrating them. He may fall even deeper into the trap of the atmosphere than the injured first generation, who still have a relation with the original trauma.

Chapter 6

The impact of collective societal traumas on subsequent generations

Born into the atmosphere

It is very difficult to exit from the atmosphere, although not impossible. Family members drawn into the atmosphere – members of both the traumatized first generation and the following generation – experience the exiting of any family member, of any endeavor to separate, as if they had to relinquish a vital organ. Every person drawn in feels unable to live without the other, experiences that separation as unsurvivable – so maintaining the atmosphere is a question of survival for the family.

Maintaining the atmosphere is in the interest of the next generation too, because only in the atmosphere can they experience intimacy and closeness with their otherwise lonely parent who retreats into the intrasubjective world: the atmosphere is the only way to relate in families with transgenerational trauma. The price of the relationship, or closeness, is being drawn in, being stuck in the deadened feelings of the atmosphere, where the child has very little scope for action.

Basic mistrust

As we have seen, as the result of severe, unintegratable trauma, the traumatized person's relationship to the world is damaged. Basic trust is replaced by basic mistrust (or the basic fault; Balint, 1979, 1999). In the case of societal traumas this feeling is the shared experience of an entire social group (Virág, 1999, 283), and its impact is thus deeper and longer term, with the traumatic life-world being validated: what the environment mirrors is that the intrasubjective reality experienced by the trauma victim is genuine reality. For the traumatized individual and the traumatized community, the traumatic life-world becomes permanent, and defines how members of the group react to internal (psychic) and external (relational, real) events.

For the next generation who are born into the transgenerational atmosphere, and who share the parents' life-world, there is basic mistrust by default, and this defines their relationship to the world and others. For them, the familiar

world of the atmosphere represents security – while this experiential field preserves a hibernated version of the original experience of the trauma. The
threatening contents are enclosed in an inner capsule, a part of the self, and
cannot be integrated by either the trauma victim or the heir as their own
experience; instead, they are projected onto the external world and external
relationships. Thus, the threat of the external world becomes fixed and permanent. Because of this, the heirs can perceive the external world, the current
here-and-now, and any relationship that would distance them from the world
of the atmosphere, as dangerous.

Children not born for their own sake

Memorial candle or replacement children is the term given to the children born
after the war who unconsciously are born with the mission of living the lives
of their siblings murdered during the Holocaust, of replacing them, of filling
the gap left by them (Wardi, [1992], 1995; Bárdos et al., 1995; Anisfeld and
Richards, 2000, 303–305). The children, who are often unaware of the existence of the lost sibling, are not able to live their own lives. Their unconscious
mission is to give their parents a meaning to life again: in other words, to
keep alive their "dead" parents, who are severely psychologically damaged
because of the unprocessed mourning. Their mission, however, is impossible to
realize, because for the survivor parents the ideal child continues to be the
dead, unmourned child ("the ideal child is a dead child"; Schwab, 2009,
281–284), so the gap caused by the loss can never be filled by the "memorial
candle" children.

The "memorial candle child" does not preserve the loss as a memory: the
child is the memory itself. The child is a witness, whose very existence bears
testimony. The part of the parent's self, split off due to the trauma, and preserving the unintegrated experiences, becomes a part of the child's own self
through transmission. The dead sibling or family member, and the undigested
contents associated with the trauma and the loss, live on as a sealed part of the
self for both the parent and the child. While the child attempts to fulfill its
mission (preserving the part of the self), the loss can be considered not to have
happened. However, in reality, this is what makes it unmourned and hence
permanent.

In large societal traumas, where the trauma is shared by a whole generation,
the common mission of following generations may be to preserve the memory
of the trauma in unsymbolized form, by their very existence. The expanded
we-experience at the group level carries not a concrete traumatic experience of
a lost family member, but the loss experience of a generation. The members of
the following generations preserve as a memorial candle not (or not only) the
losses of their ancestors, but the loss of the entire traumatized generation.

As we saw earlier, the parent takes refuge from the unprocessable loss in
a hibernated state of suspended animation in an intrasubjective world far from

the external world, into which she draws the child. At the same time, the birth of the child provokes the hibernated state. Its vitality brings a new and disturbing quality of experience into the parent's life. For the parent, the child is dangerous, being continually in interaction with the world, building its own self, making attempts at separation, and having separated from the mother wants to be itself. By drawing the child into the transgenerational atmosphere, the parent avoids having to live under the constant threat of continually existing, changing, and interacting with the external world. In order to defend herself against unbearable anxiety, that once out in the world the child will be "lost" to her, the parent gives birth only in the physical sense; psychologically the child remains captive in the intrasubjective space. The parent does not allow it to grow up with its own personality, to separate, because for her the child is an important part of the self, necessary for survival. The parent does not allow the child to flee from this shared existence experience, from this mode of relatedness, because an attempt at separation arouses in her disintegration anxieties, as if a part of her were being ripped out: for her, separation is equivalent to death.

The parent relives the relationship with the dead lost world in the relationship with the child. On a conscious level she communicates that she is living in order for the child to live, and to be happy, but the child's experience is that it cannot live its own life, it must be partly dead – it is unchanging, not itself, but somebody to carry the lost ones. It cannot meet the parent's expectations either way: if it identifies with the lost family member ("just like him") it calls forth the unprocessed loss experience from the parent. If it is "different from him" then it does not fulfill the memorial candle function: it does not preserve the loss, and thus "kills" the lost child or family member. Zoltán, aged 65, spoke of this as follows:

> "I wasn't allowed to live. The sense of guilt prevented me having my own life. My mother didn't let me go. I didn't understand why I can't live. It wasn't me. I didn't have a personality. A part of me was dead. [...] I vegetated. I too [...] was in non-existence, in a terrible death, like my mother. [...] It wasn't just that I wasn't free to live. Living was forbidden. So that I wouldn't see the loveless state she was living in. She didn't want me to witness that deadened existence that she was."

The children not born for their own sake remain a part of the self of the parent. Without their own stable core self, as a part of the self, they are genuinely unable to live without the parent. They too live in a deadened state, though the sensation of this is dynamically different to that of the first generation. Independent, the child is not able to experience himself as complete, as living: he needs relationships. But this means dependent, rather than mature relatedness: he needs the parent as the core self, and the atmosphere as a shared experiential field. Later the relationship with the parent can be replaced by other relationships, which, however, will very likely be dependent relationships, and fit into the atmosphere: the relationships serve to keep him alive. This may be a relationship with a partner, or with the child heir (of the third generation, then the next), who likewise is born as an auxiliary self-object, for survival.

The relationship to reality, distortion of space-time in the subsequent generations

As we have seen, a severely traumatized individual creates an experiential field, an intrasubjective space in which and through which the events of the past, the danger, the sense of threat, are expanded into the present. The moment of trauma is frozen, and becomes constant, timeless. The next generation is drawn into this intrasubjective world, in which the *here-and-now* reality is that of the parents, their surreal world preserving the hibernated traumatic event. For them the default time is that of trauma: the experience of linearity (life events come one after another and link up) is replaced by circularity (the same thing constantly repeated). For the survivor, spatial and temporal disorientation is a basic experience: it is impossible to know what happens when, and to whom.

Viktória is a 30-year-old third-generation Holocaust survivor. Her maternal grandparents and her paternal grandfather survived the Holocaust concentration camps. They told her very little about this period. Viktória's paternal grandmother, when she was a young girl, went into hiding in the countryside, while the others were deported. She never speaks of her memories or of her life before the Holocaust.

Viktória is currently a final year student at university, and just before her exams she collapses, falling into a state of utter desperation. As things turns out she performs well, but while she's waiting for the results she doesn't admit this to herself. She believes that if she feels something has gone badly, and she "falls apart", then the exams might go well after all. If she were satisfied with her performance, she imagines she'd fail. After the success, following a short breather, everything starts over: another challenge, another collapse, another deadline she has to wait for, and on which everything depends – her whole life, she says.

The life of the family is haunted by constant anxiety, and concrete and undefined guilt. Viktória's father, who is continually worrying and anxious about family members, considers himself responsible for the death of his parents: he couldn't be reached by telephone when needed. Viktória too feels she always has to be available, just in case there's a problem. Viktória and her brother keep an irrationally close relationship with their parents, and one of them always has to be available for them. As brother and sister, they share it between them. Viktória calls the shared experience of the family members "common sense".

Members of the following generations drawn into the atmosphere experience the world as split, as if they were living in two parallel universes. The frozen world of the past and the reality of the present are both simultaneously existing realities. For Viktória, the psychic reality is loneliness and the constantly recurrence of almost psychotic collapses. Over and over, she comes out of the paralyzed, hibernated, quasi-dead state, and is filled with life and energy. Like the phoenix, she burns up everything, razing herself to the ground, dying of her wounds, so that for a short while she will have the right to be reborn, to live. For her this dynamic is so natural, and the state so familiar, that it was only during therapy that she started to discern this.

Viktória's grandparents experienced the Holocaust, a reality not possible to integrate. The processing of the loss and pain surpasses the processing ability of their psychic apparatus. For them the unintegrated reality became reality, and this surreal, frozen traumatic experience was transmitted through the atmosphere to the following generations.

Viktória, did not experience these traumatic events herself, indeed she has barely an idea of what her grandparents went through from snatches of conversation "accidentally" overheard; but for her the grandparents' life-world, with its surreal quality, is reality. She is unable, or able only in certain cases, to react to the genuine events in the external world. Over and over she is sucked into the life-world of the past, the transgenerational trauma. For her, continuity is provided predominantly by the *we*-experience, which defines the present, her affective experience, her attitude to relationships, and her relationship to the external world.

Parallelism

As we saw earlier, an individual who has experienced a severe societal trauma protects himself from the affectively destructive impact of the experience by splitting. While he has a real life, (learning a trade, making a living, getting married, etc.) there exists another parallel inner arena, in which the traumatized existence lives on, even if this is never shared verbally with anybody. The next generation inherits both worlds. They perceive a reality where they (the next generation) are active, perhaps even successful, while through the atmosphere they experience the hidden world too.

In the next vignette the deep unprocessable experience of loss and loneliness, unexpressed in words, appears only in dreams.

Anna, a second-generation Holocaust survivor, describes this state as "dual existence". During the day she is successful, bright, and cheerful, and manages her life well. But at night she seems to arrive in "another world", where all is hopeless, dead, lonesome. At such times she feels the other reality does not exist. She has a recurrent dream: she is alone in a scorched, dead landscape. She is not scared; she knows there is nothing to fear – nobody now exists but her. Although she is aware of the existence of the other, real world, she is unable to relate to it.

In order for Anna to be able to live, for her *here-and-now me*-experiences to find room, she splits the anxiety and feeling of deadness – the *we*-experience – from her daytime, conscious existence. The feelings banished to the unconscious can thus only appear at night. With this psychic mechanism, Anna lives in both worlds.

Guilt and shame

The second- and third-generation survivor very soon is faced by the fact that the parent is basically cheerless, introverted, difficult to reach emotionally. Or, although the survivor lives a "normal" life, from time to time she is overcome by a deep state of fear and anxiety, which comes as if from nowhere.

Already as a child, the heir has to confront the fact that he is unable to resolve this. With his *me*-centered childlike thinking, he feels responsible for it. The heir carries this guilt almost from his birth. The guilt prompts him to make atonement. He experiences the atonement as a mission taking priority over all else. It is more important than finding himself, than creating an independent self. Thus, the guilt is a barrier to the development of autonomy, to the creation of an autonomous self.

The following generations wrestle with deeply embedded, almost irresolvable guilt, which become a part of the personality. Its psychological origin is probably manifold, and only partly explained by their parents' survival guilt. As we saw earlier, the child preserves the traumatic experience in a psychological capsule, a self-deposit. In this sealed part of the self, which preserves undigested and undifferentiated complexes of sensations, the traumatic experience, the feelings of the victims may be preserved; even the feelings, undifferentiated, of the perpetrator can be preserved. This sealed part of the self is shared and thus becomes part of the child's own self, so it may be activated by a current life situation, particularly one associated with loss or separation. Thus, difficult feelings such as shame and guilt may inexplicably "latch on" to many relationship events in the following generations. Zoltán speaks of this:

> "Guilt is in me all the time. As if it were the basis of all my feelings. It permeates everything about me. That may be the reason I'm not able to defend myself against anyone. It's as if their hurting me were my punishment. Because of my guiltiness, I often subject myself to others. Surprisingly, I experience this as something that lessens the feeling of guilt in me.
>
> When I said it permeates my being, it's really as if I feel I can't be happy, or successful. I have no right to be. I don't actually know why. It's like an axiom. That's the way it is. It can't be questioned. The sinner should suffer. Because I'm a sinner, it's natural that I have to suffer. That's the way it's been all my life."

In the extract above, another function of guilt can be found: this difficult feeling is part of the relationship with the parent, and itself preserves a memory. The parent finds release from unbearably difficult feelings such as shame and guilt, by depositing them in the child, as an external part of the self. She transmits and shares with him a memory both painful and verbally inexpressible. For the child, separating from the guilt may mean separating from and thus "killing" the parent.

Anxiety

The first-generation trauma victim can link feelings to an object, in other words a previous experience; the feelings may be terrifying, threatening, triggering anxiety, but they are not impalpable, not totally foreign to reality.

The following generation, born into the transgenerational atmosphere, encounters simultaneously both this unbearably present state, and the fact that they do not know what to link it to. They "believe" the ancestors, that the danger, the threat, actually exists. They experience feelings unrelated to their own life events and stories, and these feelings emerge via the transmitting milieu of the atmosphere. One patient describes the following scenario: "The experience isn't mine, but I know the feeling. That is mine too. I'm the carrier of my father's feeling."

The atmosphere transmits an object-less, continuous, constantly present visceral anxiety to the next generation. Another patient described this as follows:

> "It's as if I were seeing the world with my father's eyes, as if I were experiencing the external world through his experience. Sometimes he is in me, or I am in him, it's impossible to follow, but one thing is sure: the bond is unbreakable. Anxiety is a very deep feeling in me. It is part of me, like my hand or my foot. A permanent fixture."

Remembering and narrative

As we have seen, for subsequent generations there is often no explanation for the parents' behavior, only the behavior itself, the parents' reaction to certain words or situations to provide a model (Cserne et al., 1989; Mészáros, 1990, 33; Szilágyi et al., 1992, 121–124; Pető, 2014, 219–221). Shut out from a narrative, traumatic experiences are transmitted via other channels, mostly unconsciously, for instance as a behavior or as somatic sensations. The following case excerpt is an example.

After three years of analytically oriented therapy, Rebeka reaches a stage where she identifies the fear she experiences in unexpected situations in proximity to aggressive people.

"Nowadays I'm beginning to discern what is playing out in me before my fear reaction. Panic-stricken alarm, followed by numbness. I can hardly move. I feel that something terrible is going to happen. This is triggered by unexpected noises, or coarse behavior.

I've been thinking about where it might come from, and so powerfully. I sense that this strong reaction is unwarranted. Then suddenly I recognized it from somewhere. First, I just felt in my body, it came from there, my grandfather's house, dark, frozen in time. With them [her grandparents], if a car stopped in front of the house, they stood motionless and listened. If I spoke to them, they snapped at me to stay mum. I remember I began to be frightened. Then everything went on as usual, but the tensions hung there in the air, and in me too. I know that's how the secret police took off my grandfather, they came in a car and took him. The family heard nothing of him for months. Somehow I always knew this, and yet I didn't. But I'd never linked up the two: the fear, the terror I felt in my body, and the experience at my grandfather's place."

In Rebeka's family they couldn't talk about what they feared, having a family member taken away, so the fear was passed down in the child, as a visceral anxiety. In Rebeka's case one key difference with the previous cases is that she had her own experience of the event, albeit unverbalized. Perhaps that is why the original trauma was more accessible.

The memory of several societal traumas can sometimes be completely driven out of the narrative. When there is no verbal conveying, and there are no memories, at least on the symbolized level, the transgenerational atmosphere may become the only form of remembering and of sharing the experience. The subsequent generations receive as their inheritance uncontainable, unsymbolized emotions, with this form of transmission of the experience replacing narrative. This experience, already traumatic, is thus also the history of the family. It is a memory of the people, of the world, that disappeared. Márta, a second-generation Holocaust survivor, presented with the following dream:

"I'm in a beautiful, vivacious city, Paris perhaps. I meet my girlfriend, and we go to a wellness hotel. She suggests we go to a very good restaurant. I get tense, wondering whether I have enough time. After all, she knows I've come from the death-camp, and I have to get back in time. Otherwise there might be big trouble for the folk I've left behind."

Exiting the atmosphere, the we-experience is equivalent to forgetting, which on the one hand threatens the disintegration of the patient's own (childlike) self, and on the other threatens to "kill" the parents, and family members involved in the atmosphere. Márta got only temporary leave from the suffocating world of the atmosphere, and she has to return, or else "there might be trouble for the folk she's left behind".

The child remembers by existing; in other words, the child itself is the memory. At the same time, children of survivors often feel that their memories are patchy, and they recall their own childhoods in a fragmentary manner. This can perhaps be explained by the fact that for the generations drawn into the atmosphere, continuity and self-continuity is provided by the *we*-experience. In line with this the experiences and memories are inserted into the self-narrative alongside the *we*-experience. Meanwhile there are some *me*-experiences and personal memories quite different in quality. Pleasant, good experiences are, however, very difficult to integrate with the oppressive, threatening feelings aroused by the atmosphere. These *me*-experiences do not easily slot into the *we*-narrative, so are either forgotten, or it is hard to locate them in space and time, and their insertion into the self-narrative is fragmentary.

Continuity

In the case of severe societal traumas, the post-trauma intrasubjective life-world becomes permanent, hibernates, and for the subsequent generations it is predominantly this state of suspended animation, this traumatized life-world, the *we*, that gives continuity. At the same time the survivor has a relationship with the external world, albeit fleetingly, and the continuity represented by the current reality appears. This duality of continuity haunts the lives of the following generations: to any real or perceived threat the survivor unconsciously retreats into the traumatic life-world, the continuity of *we*.

The second and third generations thus experience continuity predominantly on the basis of the *we*-experience. It is in this continuity that the child relates to the experiences of the trauma victim – this will be the life-world that provides the connection, the link between generations.

The feelings carried in the *we*-experience, such as anxiety, guilt, loss, and loneliness, are a part of the continuity experience. Paradoxically, these difficult feelings represent security: continuity with the trauma victim and with the past, when memories are otherwise unutterable.

For subsequent generations, continuity means fixation in the traumatic experience. In this respect, the second-third-generation individual is, in the words of one subject, like a "carrier", who passes on the experience of the trauma victim.

Imagination

As we saw earlier (see the section *Imagination* in chapter 3) the trauma as a surreal reality deprives the individual of the *as-if*-reality of imagination, and the boundary between reality and imagination becomes blurred. The fears experienced by the trauma victim are projected onto the present and become permanent. The experience of the past (which is not a memory, but the reality of the present) carries a constant threat.

Healthy imagination, which enables us to play with reality and fantasy, and to pass between the two worlds, is replaced by distorted imagination. The world of distorted imagination is actually the surreal reality of the trauma. This is a world in which there is no sharp boundary between past, present, and future, between fantasy and reality; all attempts at fantasy harbor a risk.

The child is unable to navigate between the fantasized world created by distorted imagination and the real world. Attempts at fantasy threaten to bring the loss of the ability to orient oneself in time and space, and thus also the ability to maintain a relationship with reality, ending in collapse. For the child, security is provided by the parent's perspective – the *we*-experience. Yet by identifying with the *we*-experience the child will be the emotional carrier of a traumatic experience it did not actually live through or suffer directly. Through micro scenes, via several "channels" the parent transmits his/her inner, anxious world to the child. Since she carries this dreaded state in her body, as Mihály Bálint writes (1999), the transmission may take place through touch, body aroma, posture, or a cold-warm bodily sensation. The child takes on the parent's emotional state without knowing anything about it. With the child locked in a bodily experience, its psychological scope for action is restricted: it carries anxiety at a visceral level, so the anxiety of adventure in the fantasy world is unbearable, because the child experiences the threat that fantasy will become real.

Relationship characteristics

Me or we: forbidden separation in subsequent generations

A part of my self has died. I often wanted to resuscitate the dead part of me, but it wasn't possible. The role of the dead part was to be dead. It preserved something, even when dead. Some pain, something unutterable. [...] Part of my essence is dead, and if that is in the foreground, for instance because of some injury, then I want to destroy myself, like my mother did with me. At such times I steer clear of folk, so there is no witness or victim to the way I operate. At such times I can disappear. As if I didn't exist. At these times I have no living relationship with anyone at all. It's a strange, alien, but familiar state.

With Zoltán, we see that his seriously traumatized mother, a Holocaust survivor, transmitted the trauma via two channels: one, partly through her inability to provide a secure attachment for her son, she was unable to contain the feelings overwhelming the child and herself, and two, partly through the atmosphere into which the child was born. The boy experienced on the one hand that his mother was unable to let him go, while at the same time hating him (this is a relationship experience he lived through personally), and on the other, through the atmosphere she shared the deadness, the unsymbolized traumatic experience with her son – who then felt this experience to be his own. Later in his own life, in his own relationships, Zoltán creates what his mother created for him, and what the trauma created for his mother. This is no mere repetition of trauma: for him and for them this sharing of experience is one form of relatedness, perhaps the only form.

For those living in the atmosphere, independent relationship experiences that take them outside the shared relationship field are not permitted. As we pointed out earlier, "exiting" represents a dual threat for subsequent generations. On the one hand it "kills" the bearer of the trauma, by depriving them of the meaning of life: living for their child. On the other hand, for the traumatized second-generation, unable to live without the parental self, maintaining the atmosphere is necessary also because it is only through this that they can experience intimacy with the parent, who is otherwise alone and often inaccessible in their own trauma.

The price of this proximity is mimicry, a hibernated existence, in which the child has no scope for action, and can move only in the extremely restrictive system of reference of the transgenerational atmosphere. The shared transgenerational self-experience is important to the family as a mode of both relating and attachment. For Zoltán, the *we*-identity created by his mother is still present today:

> "… I always felt that I could be hers alone. That was my destiny, to live for her. If I had some endeavor to be my own self, I prevent it. Even in my relationships, I can only be in them for a short while. I feel that if I were my own self, I would cease to be. I lug my mother around with myself like she used to haul her memories of Auschwitz. Invisible, but indivisibly attached."

The heir feels that he is there for the parent. The need to belong together may be stronger than the need for independent existence. At other times, this belonging together and merging, and the desire for separation, may be in conflict with one another. First one, then the other will be dominant, or compromise situations will form, for instance, short-term relationships with others.

The transgenerational atmosphere defines the second- and third-generations' own important relationships too. The descendant draws his partner into the atmosphere just as his parent did with him. He chooses a partner that "fits into" the family atmosphere. Thus, the new relationship does not threaten an exit from the earlier relationship mode, which for him is the only conceivable form of relatedness. He does not truly relate to the other, but he expects the other to fit into the atmosphere.

The state of readiness becomes permanent

Survivor families are characterized by a permanent state of readiness, and recurrent crisis situations are then successfully resolved. For the second generation the state of readiness conjuring up the life-world of the original traumatic event is the default state, as they are born into it; later, they draw their partner into it (as their default mode of operation), and then their children. The child fitting into the *we*-experience, satisfying the parents' need to save it, continually presents problems: the child produces somatic symptoms necessitating a rush trip to the doctor, or it is psychologically fragile, demanding the heightened presence of the parent.

Aggression

Zoltán told of an experience he had at the age of 14:

> "I no longer remember what started it. Nothing powerful. Perhaps I didn't immediately do what she asked. My mother pitched into me, giving me a good thrashing. And she shouted: 'You little runt. If I say do it, then you do it.' I don't remember the rest. That 'little runt' still resounds in my head. I thought she was going to kill me. After a while she shoved me into the larder. I was there for hours in the dark. I didn't know when I'd be let out. Something died in me then. My soul, I think. When she let me out, she behaved as if she'd just chastised me a bit, as if I'd been in the larder for a minute. 'You'll obey mummy from now on, won't you?' she said in that affected tone I knew so well. To me, this meant: behave as if nothing had happened."

For those who experience societal traumas, the repression of aggression is very powerful, but its splitting off is far more typical. Several mechanisms may play a role in the dynamic of managing aggression. One is identification with the aggressor, which is basically repressed, but another mechanism cited earlier (Volkan, 2013, 233) is possible: stored in the split-off and sealed self-deposit there may be even the image of the aggressor, which is actually the unsymbolized memory of the aggression, of the relationship with the aggressor. However, the images and sensations that have been split off and cling together (including aggression and the image of the aggressor) may sometimes burst flash-like into the consciousness of the individual, and the survivor may change into a cruel aggressor. At such times the feelings stored in the part of the self hermetically sealed off from other parts may break free and overwhelm the trauma victim. The parent later experiences this flash as if it had not happened, like Zoltán's mother in the excerpt above. The feeling disappears again, and waits for the next opportunity.

For the next generation, the parent's reaction is incomprehensible, disproportionate, and unidentifiable. They feel the harsh relationship event to be independent of them, unexpected and uncontrolled. For the child, this flash experience represents an encounter both with the vulnerability, the beaten state, of the traumatized parent, and also the parent's aggression directed at him. This experience makes him witness and victim at one and the same time.

The following generation feels they cannot express aggression. As Zoltán put it: he has to behave as if nothing had happened. The message they get from the trauma victim is: don't be aggressive, because that threatens the parent, it can "kill" her. Indeed, for the parent, the mirroring back of her own aggression is unbearable.

For the heir, a further difficulty may be that the milieu of the atmosphere transmits the parent's own split-off parts in a direct manner, undigested. The purpose of the deposit is for the traumatized parent to rid themselves of the unbearably painful images and emotions (Volkan, 2013, 233). The child is thus confronted not only with the parental aggression, but may encounter foreign, overwhelming sensations within his own self. This means the origin of the aggression overwhelming him is unknown to him: the aggressive sensations in his own relationship experience and in his self-deposit may form such an unprocessed mass of sensation that it cannot be integrated into the self-narrative, so the necessary defense is to repress it, or rather to split it off, as though it never happened.

As *me*-identity grows, the repressed behaviorial elements that were forbidden, repressed, split off in the *we*-identity begin to appear. The *me* that endeavors to separate would like to integrate all the split-off parts, including aggression. This process is part of the construction of an independent self, an accessory to an autonomous process. However, separation, and with it the taking on of the split-off parts, including aggression, is not allowed in the atmosphere. The heir, who is compelled to dissemble the aggression directed at the parent, and who initially finds no object for it, may later cling with a disproportionate feeling to a person, a life situation, projecting onto the external world the uncontainable feelings welling up in him/her.

Containment

As we saw in the section *The Loss of basic trust*, due to trauma the parent's ability to contain and delay is severely compromised. She is not able to contain the *here-and-now* relationship with the child. External experiences (from the child) and internal (split-off) experiences overwhelm the parent. She is unable to provide either the child or herself with protection against anxiety or difficult feelings. For both of them, the transitional space, the containment, is replaced by the atmosphere. However, the atmosphere as a milieu makes them ill in several ways. Certain feelings it is unable to contain, and it distorts others. In the atmosphere there is no place for the child to have feelings such as anger or aggression, while other feelings are over-emphasized, such as anxiety.

The child, confronted with the fact the parent is unable to contain the feelings overwhelming her, makes an attempt to contain the feelings overwhelming the parent, and tries to become a parent to the parent. Both of them experience failure, a failure of the ability to contain.

Mirroring

In the case of a healthy relationship, the role of the mother is to mirror the child (Winnicott, [1971], 1999). Damage to the mother's holding function, to her ability to mirror and contain, result in damage to the early idealization and attachment needs. This leads to early damage to the self, such as reduced tolerance of tension, strong dissociative tendencies, growing fragmentation, identity disorders, and the operation of the false self.

The creation and maintenance of inner self-cohesion in the child requires not only the mirror function of the mother, but a good enough milieu, which is able to contain and mirror the parent as a human being. In societal traumas the individual has the sense that the image mirrored by the external world in its role as a "mirroring mother" conveys the message "I am unacceptable to society" – an image which cannot be integrated, so the individual's own mirroring function is damaged. She retreats into an internal reality, the atmosphere, and later this is what she mirrors to her child, instead of internal and external reality.

The traumatized mother (parent) is unable to contain or mirror either the reality of the present, or the child's internal world and feelings. Instead of the *here-and-now* reality, the threatening world of the past is mirrored, while intersubjective relatedness with the child is replaced by intrasubjective relatedness, which does not mirror the child.

After trauma, when the damaged parent is unable either to healthily contain or to mirror the child, the roles of the generations may be reversed. It may become the role, the mission, of the wise baby (Ferenczi, [1933], 2006b, 101–112) to mirror the parent, the parent's existence: to make the "dead" mother live. In transgenerational trauma, it is not the child that sees itself mirrored back in its mother's eyes, but what the mother expects to see, mirrored in her child's eyes: the fact that she lives, that she exists (see the section *Children not born for their own sake*).

For the second generation the basic question "can I be myself, can I want anything?" does not even arise, because of the very early damage to mirroring. The child, who has become a mirror itself, will be unable to see or recognize itself. What remains is the early self-definition, as it saw itself in the distorted intrasubjective mirror of the parent. This mirror sometimes signals emptiness, sometimes danger – the parent has a faulty relationship with reality, and these feelings too are projected onto reality.

Chapter 7

Therapeutic aspects of transgenerational trauma

Observations from therapy in the Holocaust literature

We highlight some observations in the literature which describe therapy work with Holocaust survivors and their descendants, with its special features and difficulties. Later, we attempt to dovetail all these observations into the theoretical framework of the transgenerational atmosphere.

Survivor syndrome

William G. Niederland was the first to describe the complex clinical syndrome observable in the survivors of concentration camps and other similarly serious, prolonged, and collective traumas, which he called survivor syndrome. He described the syndrome as including chronic depression and anxiety, sleeping disorders, the appearance of nightmares, cognitive and memory disorders, a change in personality, a tendency towards isolation, symptoms of a psychotic nature, identity disorders, psychosomatic disorders, and a "living corpse" appearance (Niederland, 1968, 313).

The therapist as persecutor

The children of survivors – intelligent young folk with a good upbringing – are often mistrustful during therapy, like their parents: They are liable to experience the therapist as a persecutor, and this mistrust can transform into resistance of enormous proportions (Jucovy, 1985, 34–37, 1992, 269–269, 1994, 14–16, 25; Virág, 1996, 28). This negative reaction to therapy can be linked to the parents' (unspoken) past of persecution, to the fear of intrusion. The patient may experience the apparently fair, early interpretations as intrusion, and they may therefore be harmful. Therapy with survivors and their descendants is not easy, hides many traps, and demands particular discretion. The temptation is great for the therapist to cast themselves in the role of savior, which can, however, hamper the formation of negative transference. In addition, Holocaust patients can mobilize very strong escape fantasies in the therapist. The cautious dosage and timing of therapy interventions is of crucial importance, and the handling of secrets is of special significance, particularly secrets arising during analysis (Jucovy, 1985, 42–48, 1992, 275–279, 1994, 23–28).

Kestenberg also recounts the difficulties experienced during therapy, for instance the highly ambivalent attachment model of a child survivor, who, expecting the analyst to let him down, left the relationship himself (Kestenberg, 1994, 86); and in another case, when the patient cast doubt on the therapist's professional identity. Behind the exclusion of the therapist, there may lie the trauma of being excluded: through identification with the aggressor the patient excludes others (ibid., 92).

On the challenges and special features of therapy with second- and third-generation survivors, Virág writes: "The pseudo-psychotic patient sees a persecutor in everyone, even in the analyst. Descendants of survivors are particularly sensitive to negative transference." For this reason, it is wise to treat deep interpretation very cautiously, as it can reinforce paranoid fantasies (Virág, 1996, 28). A therapeutic goal is for the patient to be able to see, in his persecuting parents, the memory of the one who persecuted his parents (Virág, 1996, 24). In the magical "mother-mirror" the child sees not just the mother, but the external world; he sees mirrored the mother's own preverbal memories. Virág points out that if "the analyst's attention does not extend to the 'external world-mother', the processing of hostile feelings towards the mother will likely be hampered, and may become impossible.[…] The goal of therapy is to find the continuity of the family story in the individual's symptoms." (Virág, 1996, 72).

The telescoping of generations

Faimberg (2005, 4–30, 42–49) explains some characteristics of the therapy with the phenomenon of transgenerational telescoping (or the compression of several generations), such as the appearance of emptiness and absence in transference-counter-transference, or the enigmatic negative therapeutic reaction. She points out that questions related to the identity and identifications of the patient cannot, or only with difficulty, be understood from his life story alone; listening to the patient's own voice from out of the telescoped life-world of several generations demands a special therapeutic attitude (Faimberg, 2005, 19–30). The "survivor complex" posited by Kestenberg refers to a similar phenomenon, the telescoping of experiences of generations: the children of survivors tend to identify with the parent, and with the parent's past (Kestenberg, 1980, 802–803, 1994, 84, 93).

In her article 'Kút és műhely. A holocaust-szindróma megjelenése a pszichoterápiás gyakorlatban' [Well and workshop. The appearance of Holocaust syndrome in psychotherapeutic practice], Virág recounts how the "terrible influx of the past into the present can manifest itself as a psychotic state in the second generation." (Virág, 1994, 135).

The phantom – an alien body in the therapeutic space

Ábrahám tells of how the phantom, which "enters the unconscious of the child from that of the parent" is difficult to manage with the "classic tools of analysis".

> Thus, the phantom cannot even be recognized by the subject as evident in an 'aha' experience and, during analysis, can only give rise to constructions with all their attendant uncertainties. The phantom may nevertheless be deconstructed by analytic construction, though this occurs without the patients having the impression that they were in fact the subject of the analysis. It is clear that, in contrast to other types of cases, this work requires a genuine partnership between patient and analyst, the more so since the construction arrived at in this way bears no direct relation to the patient's own topography but concerns someone else's.
> (Abraham and Torok, 1994, 174; Ábrahám, [1975, 1987], 2001, 69)

> The phantom will vanish", he writes, "only when its radically heterogeneous nature with respect to the subject is recognized, a subject to whom it at no time has any direct reference" (ibid.). In the case of the "phantom" the classic analytic relationship and interpretation is wrong and may lead to "patients' displaced acceptance of the phantom as a part of their own libidinal life, which could in turn lead to bizarre and even delirious acts.
> (Abraham and Torok, 1994, 176; Ábrahám, [1975, 1987], 2001, 70)

The drawing in of the therapist

Many scholars write of the therapist's difficulty: being drawn into the scenic memory of the transgenerational trauma as it appears in the therapeutic space. Extreme trauma is transmitted to the following generation primarily nonverbally, and may then be transmitted in a similar manner to the therapist. The therapeutic handling and interpretation of scenic processes, often at the level of somatic sensations, is a challenge for the therapist. The scenic memories brought by the patient may activate the therapist's own transgenerational scenic memory (Grünberg and Markert, 2012, 214–219). The common task is to decode somatic sensations, feelings, and enactments, to translate scenic experiences into the language of words (Grünberg and Markert, 2012; Feldman, 2015).

Therapeutic aspects of the transgenerational atmosphere

We too have encountered similar therapeutic difficulties in our work with survivors of transgenerational trauma and their children. In the following sections we shall place the therapy experiences of the cited authors, and our own, in the theoretical framework of the transgenerational atmosphere and, based on this, further on we will put forward a suggestion for altering therapy technique.

Transgenerational transference and countertransference

During our work with the heirs of transgenerational trauma, similarly to other therapies, there unfolds the transference-countertransference field in the customary sense. Yet in parallel with this customary dynamic there appears a second "shadow" transference and countertransference, very different to the first, one which we have termed "transgenerational transference and counter-transference". While transference and countertransference can be linked to early or later relationship experiences and life events, the transgenerational transference and countertransference cannot be linked to the patient's own life events, and the feelings remain unidentified. Furthermore, there is a feeling of disproportion: the reactions of the patient, both in external relationships and in the therapy, are out of proportion to either early relationship events or those in therapy.

When we start to interpret the transgenerational transference – the place of the atmosphere in the life-story of the individual – there often appears an almost psychotic level of regression, disintegration, and deterioration, which cannot be ascribed to either therapy events or earlier life events. This reaction can be explained by the atmosphere, which provides self-coherence to the *we*-self, which is being endangered, and which threatens the patient with the disintegration of the self. This reaction could easily be interpreted as a negative therapeutic reaction, a defense. In actual fact this is a manifestation of the primitive self-defense mechanism characteristic of the atmosphere.

The self, unable to live alone, needs the security of the *we*, so it provides an opportunity for the building of the therapeutic relationship by drawing the therapist into the atmosphere. Initially, the therapist becomes a participant in the life-world of the atmosphere; following the identification, the therapist eventually gets a better perspective and sees what is being jointly created.

In the initial stages of therapy, it is thus important that the therapist enter the transgenerational atmosphere offered by the patient, for whom this is the only way to share the transgenerational legacy in this phase. At this point, the transference-countertransference processes are dominated by transgenerational transference. The shared field makes it possible for the transgenerational trauma victim to share unsymbolized contents, creating the opportunity for shared containing. At this point the therapist does nothing but contain, or more accurately helps to contain the split-off, dissociated feeling and self-states. Later, as therapy progresses, as the patient is able to experience his own autonomous self-sensations and the object-self relationship appears emotionally, the therapist can give greater emphasis to transference and countertransference in the classic sense (complementary and concordant counter-transference, the idealized object, etc.) and work with them.

In the earlier section entitled *The relationship to reality, distortion of space-time in the subsequent generations* we referred to Viktória's therapy. In her therapy the mutual trust which formed at the start was replaced as therapy went on by a feeling of vulnerability, loneliness, in the countertransference, helplessness, and guilt. This dual transference, a combined transference based on the self-experience and the transgenerational transference, is thereafter continually present, and at every session we build our relationship anew – similarly to the experience of Viktória "dying" in every exam, to rise reborn like a phoenix from destruction for a short while. In countertransference the visceral feeling of guilt and hopelessness is so strong it is often unclear to whom it belongs. Although Viktória suffers from constant anxiety and tormenting guilt, which cannot be associated with an actual event or her personal experience, or the close, symbiotic relationship with her family, all attempts at interpreting this prompt a paradoxical effect: she grows distant, retreating into a lonely regressive state, or simply does not hear the interpretations. Later she says that this anxious, guilty feeling, though tormenting, is important to her. For her, it is unconceivable that she would separate from it: the very thought fills her with mortal dread. For her this feeling represents the family, and important relationships.

Seeking the root of the transference feelings, such as vulnerability, loneliness, the experiences that would correspond to these, cannot be found in Viktoria's personal life history. And yet, the basic experience of anxiety and guilt has haunted her since she was a small child, it has influenced her important relationships, and in time it occurs in the therapy relationship.

Her apparently paradoxical reaction to the interpretation can be understood through the transgenerational self-experience: the incipient differentiation, "healing" of her own self-part threatens both the *we*-self and her own self, whose existence depends on the *we*, the transgenerational self. Because the *we* (and the *me*) feel under attack, apparently uncontrollable primitive defense mechanisms come into action. As Viktória put it, for her these feelings represent the family, and important relationships. It is unthinkable that she would leave behind these feelings. The thought of separation fills her with mortal fear.

Almost destructive transference-countertransference feelings reminiscent of work with psychotic patients can prompt therapists to defend themselves, since very intense and threatening feelings are deeply provocative to the boundaries of the therapist's self (Bion, 1959). The therapy space is overwhelmed by the atmosphere, an important part of which is transgenerational defense (and splitting); the therapist drawn into the atmosphere also identifies with it, and tries not to let the identification permit a splitting of the difficult feelings. The temptation is great for the therapist, in an effort to protect him/herself and the therapy relationship, to proceed to a more easy-flowing state, not allowing the therapy to go deeper: instead of allowing for the uncontainable transgenerational experiences he/she proceeds to more manageable feelings.

In a supervision, a therapist presented a case that had stumped him. A 26-year-old woman was coming to him for therapy, seeking help with her deep anxiety and relationship problems. My colleague had been the woman's therapist for five years. Sometimes the patient disappeared, then turned up again. The therapist was constant, time and time again he accepted her back. The woman finished university, did well at work, but her anxiety was unresolved. During supervision we touched on her life-story, and the fact that her mother was involved in the Holocaust. The therapist had almost neglected this. Although he knew of it, he had not linked the unrealistic anxiety to the woman being a third-generation Holocaust survivor. During supervision, he expressed concern: "I felt it would be too much for us, I was worried I wouldn't know what to do with this feeling, and because of that I wouldn't be able to protect my patient either." The supervisor felt that the unconscious rejection jeopardized the patient's progress. There was a dualism of feeling: partly, he felt that the patient wasn't in good hands; partly that the patient would do well, because she was hidden, protected.

In the case above the undigested sensations of the transgenerational atmosphere probably overwhelmed the therapy space, temporarily severely limiting the therapist's container capacity. The supervisor's entry into the therapy as a third helped to restore the third function of the analyst. Only in the supervisor could the split be verbalized; together a long time, patient and therapist were both involved in the transgenerational atmosphere, protecting one another and themselves. The world of the patient, the transgenerational atmosphere, occurred in the supervisor too, but with sufficient distance from the trauma and the relationship that was permeated with the transgenerational atmosphere, the supervisor became able to verbalize this duality and splitting of worlds.

In transgenerational countertransference, the transgenerational atmosphere is present, with the almost psychotic, almost unutterable, unrepresentable traumatic *we*-experience in which the patient and the family live. Working with the transgenerational countertransference is a great challenge for the analyst. On one hand, an almost psychotic experience is shared in the analytic field, in which the defense mechanism characteristic of the patient and her family appears in the analyst too (such as denial, splitting, or projection); on the other hand, the overshadowed field may activate her own transgenerational experiences, her own "psychotic" parts. In this phase, certain aspects of the therapy resemble work with a psychotic patient – while unlike in psychosis, parallel, functioning non-psychotic self-parts exist. The therapist, defending herself, may be prone to collusion: she does not allow the therapy to go deep, to delve into the world of the transgenerational atmosphere, but steers toward an easier relationship (the classic transference-countertransference work) while the transgenerational transference is the only way for the patient to share experience. If the analyst interprets this as resistance, or avoids it, this may arouse in the patient feelings of disappointment, of not being understood, or being rejected, and thus therapist and patient perceive one another as mutually unavailable and misunderstood, and they share the feelings of disappointment and loneliness.

The "Kelemen the Mason" effect

The work of therapy, as we saw in Viktória's case, is characterized by duality. We could call this the "Kelemen the Mason" effect.

In the story of Kelemen the Mason, originating in the 1500s, the masons believe there is a curse on the castle of Déva which they are building, and that is why what they build up keeps caving in. They decide they can free themselves of the curse if they burn one of their wives, the first one to visit her husband. The ashes will then be sealed in the castle walls. The ballad has some basis in reality: the castle of Déva did indeed exist, built on a tall steep hill in Transylvania, and the ballad draws on elements of the ancient pagan religion.

Like Kelemen the mason in the story, the therapist experiences over and over that what they build up, including the therapy relationship built up earlier, caves in again and again. They are incapable of containing positive, forward-looking experiences, they cannot retain them. Positive experiences do not last, they simply disappear.

This is understandable, for with the appearance of the atmosphere of transgenerational trauma, the therapist encounters a feeling and experience alien to both herself and her patient. What is going on is incomprehensible based on the patient's earlier relationship events, and a meeting is not possible. Orientation and therapy are further hampered by the fact that the damaged parent transmits the trauma not only through the atmosphere, but at the relationship level. This early injury, often severe, appears in the therapeutic space. It can be distinguishable from the atmosphere by its being more associated with personal experiences, and more comprehensible, processable on the basis of transference-countertransference. Thus, relating with self-parts formed from genuine personal relationships, and relating with the *we*-self, often happens in alternation and unexpectedly, often in parallel, making orientation difficult for the patient and therapist. This uncertainty and slipperiness are exactly what is characteristic of the transgenerational trauma: the points of reference are lost, therapy events become incomprehensible.

Dániel, a second-generation Holocaust survivor on both sides, had been attending psychoanalytic-oriented therapy for half a year, when in order to deepen the therapy we agreed to change the setting and continue therapy twice a week with Dániel lying down. The therapist said of the experience:

> In the first phase of therapy we soon developed an informal, intimate atmosphere. Dániel was reflective and, though he struggled with embarrassment, he honestly shared very intimate and difficult experiences and fantasies. When Dániel was in the recumbent position, we seemed to arrive at a different relationship, which both of us perceived. We seemed to lose the previous therapy relationship and instead moved into another field of relationship. I had the fantasy that I lost contact with him and am left alone. I felt I became empty, that I was not able to stay in contact

with the patient. I seemed to gasp for air, and struggled to try and find the earlier relationship. I didn't understand what was happening between us. While in the seated position we understood the feelings and the events he experienced in his life history, we felt them to be proportionate and we could relate; in the recumbent position there dominated a feeling of things being disproportionate and incomprehensible.

In Dániel's case, following the change of setting, a different transference and countertransference constellation appeared, one new and alien to both patient and therapist. The more regressive position brought into the therapeutic space the previously split-off, dissociated experience of loneliness, helplessness, and emptiness, which was later possible to verbalize, and the process of integration began.

While the personal life brings forth a very colorful transference-countertrans ference field, the transgenerational countertransference is monotone and marked: the therapist, like the patient, experiences loneliness, helplessness, and emptiness. She may feel bereft of means, disappointed, feel that the other is very distant, unavailable, disappearing. She herself experiences a threatening, numbing, hibernated state. The "Kelemen the Mason" effect appears: what we build up in therapy continually caves in. Double countertransference, at the personal and transgenerational levels, may appear together, alternating one with the other. For the analyst, the sudden appearance and intensity of the transgenerational countertransference is baffling, disproportionate compared to what preceded it, and it is this surprise and lack of proportion that makes it identifiable.

Chapter 8

Methodology for the therapy of transgenerational trauma

The purpose of the therapy; therapeutic principles

As we have seen, the trauma has the effect of destroying the continuity of past, present, and future. The traumatized parent loses all hope of restoring that continuity. Subsequent generations, born as they are into the atmosphere, inherit the absence of continuity, and, as a result, a fragmentary narrative. For them, continuity means not the events of the present, but the recurrent return to the trauma, as if this for them were the beginning of time.

The aim of the therapy is, through the restoration of continuity, to create a link with the pre-trauma world, and to reduce isolation, loneliness, the hemmed-in state, and thus to strengthen the *me*, to make it more complete, continuous. Further goals, in finding a path to the narrative of past, present, and future, to emotional experience, are not only to heal the wounds caused by the trauma, but to link the pre-trauma world to the present. Also important is that the individual not relate to the family past only with the transgenerational trauma, but in its entirety.

In families with transgenerational trauma, as we saw earlier, members live in powerful symbiosis with one another. This relatedness is often like that of conjoined twins: sometimes only parts of their bodies are attached, but other times the vital organs are shared. At times the operation, although lengthy, may be successful; at other times, it is lengthy but manageable, and sometimes it is impossible to separate the twins.

In our work with transgenerational trauma we often face similar dilemmas. The goal of therapy is the construction of an autonomous and integrated self through which the individual will be able to form new, adaptive relationships with those remaining in the *we*-identity, while he also creates his own life.

At this point, the therapist must bear in mind that transgenerational therapies have their risks both for the patient and for the family members and loved ones in close symbiosis with him. Therapy takes place under the constant monitoring of how much the patient can take, and how much his important relationships can take: what can be rewritten, what for the patient is "mortally perilous", and unbearable. This is a joint process taking place mainly on the unconscious level: patient and therapist feel their way into the depth of the interventions and the speed of change together.

Work with transgenerational trauma requires a different technique to the classical analytical approach, for instance the more direct interpretation of projected contents, and the open identification of the transgenerational atmosphere as a legacy. In the first phase of therapy the therapist offers a narrative, a theoretical framework which enables the patient to differentiate between his own feelings and those of his family members, and to make separation and the severe concomitant anxiety bearable.

Alongside her validating role, the therapist represents an alternative transgenerational atmosphere – a functioning containing milieu – a part of which is her own personal (family, community) and professional identity.

As therapy proceeds the narrative offered by the therapist recedes, and more space is given to the patient's own narrative; work with the atmosphere as a given narrative is gradually replaced by a more classic mode of work, in which the emphasis is on the characteristics of the individual. Like any other approach to therapy, here too the basis of work with the atmosphere as an offered narrative is the patient's consent: in other words, he decides whether or not he can accept this narrative as a theoretical framework in which his feelings can be interpreted.

The therapy process

Miklós made an enormous effort to get on in life. Financially, professionally, and in his private life. He started several university courses, but after a time gave them up. He felt he wasn't getting on; he was out of sorts. In the hope of changing this situation, he started a course of therapy.

In the initial phase of his therapy he experienced breakdown in relation to some grievance or other. He felt he would disappear into a black hole. Meanwhile he was living and working like a zombie.

Miklós was dually present in the world. He tried to meet external demands; it was important for him not to come into conflict with anyone. If this did happen, or if he experienced a situation as conflictual, he felt unbearable fear. One such time was when at work the secretary phoned to say the boss wanted to speak to him. This 40-year-old man trembled at the thought of the meeting. He imagined being fired, of put to shame. The thought was simply devastating for him. In his behavior he attempted, mostly successfully, to conceal and hide his fears. Although he was trembling within, this was not apparent to the outside world.

He spent the initial sessions telling of similar events. In what was a long phase, I was burdened as an analyst to be present in the atmosphere of injury. As countertransference there was vulnerability, a feeling of being injured, becoming the victim. After the sessions the analyst needed time to restore her own boundaries, the security of a professional framework. From the beginning,

Miklós's reaction seemed exaggerated, out of proportion to what was going on in his life, as if he were reacting not to events in the external world, but to some internal event. It was as if the story belonged to someone else, but the emotional experience belonged to him, or perhaps to a phantom determining his emotional presence and reactions.

Therapy work with transgenerational trauma is a long process, of several years. It is tiring because both the patient and the therapist must spend much time in the state of "not knowing", together, containing the undigested sensations of several generations, until they finally become digestible, and integrable. Of help in bearing this long state of "not knowing" is the theoretical framework of the atmosphere, which we interpret not as a stasis, but as an important part of the therapeutic work (Bion, [1970], 2006, 26–40; Bezoari and Ferro, 1989; Bezoari, Ferro, and Politi, 1994).

First step: identification

In the first phase of therapy the transgenerational atmosphere is identified jointly: therapist and patient recognize that some of the experiences and feelings cannot be ascribed to personal life events – in other words they are unidentifiable from the patient's own life story. An important step in the identification process is that the patient has an exaggerated reaction to certain life situations or events; bringing his awareness to his overreaction is an important element of this phase, for both the patient and the therapist. This also helps them to understand the transference processes. As the transgenerational atmosphere unfolds, there appears the dual transference-countertransference field typical of transgenerational trauma; transference and countertransference are accompanied by transgenerational transference and countertransference. In this phase, the therapy process is characterized by an alternating forward movement and then a halting, a recurrent "getting stuck".

Even reaching out, building the relationship, is a longer process, because the analysand is basically in a *we*-state. The therapist is a threat to this *we*-state, so in the initial phase the patient, although he is physically present, in his commitment and emotional experience he maintains a considerable distance: the victim of transgenerational trauma carries a world of moods in which loneliness, sadness, loss, having no companion, and alienation are basic experiences. They experience these difficult feelings even in the therapy situation, and to conceal them, as in their other relationships, they assume an adaptive, apparently cooperative, pliable role. Although they attend the sessions regularly, their inner world is unavailable. This is why it is important that both the therapist and the patient, through identification, are clear about the impact of the transgenerational atmosphere.

In Miklós's case, it was important for him to realize that he was the heir of a transgenerational trauma, and that he intensifies the experience himself: he creates an environment in which the sense of being threatened is unbearable.

In fact, we found no personal trauma in his life history that would warrant such an intensive experience. But we found something in the family history. During analysis, it slowly emerged that his grandparents had been forced to relocate, their assets had been confiscated, and they lost their social status. Miklós inherited this trauma, and he repeatedly created this world in his real life. Identification of the root of his feelings helps to distinguish the legacy from the patient's personal involvement. In some cases it may bring great relief, if the patient is able to link a pain carried in body and soul since birth with an acute loss, crisis, or trauma, as the following excerpt shows.

Disproportion and lack of object

Ádám, 44 years old and in a divorce crisis, asks for psychotherapy help in a serious depressive state. He says the divorce has knocked him off balance.

P: I feel very great pain. I feel it's unbearable. I want to die.

T: Even at the price of death you want the suffering to stop.

P: Yes! At any price, I just want this unbearable state to end.

T: Earlier you said that these were exaggerated reactions compared to what's happened.

P: Any frustrating situation would bring out this state in me. But if I think about what my life is like, I shouldn't be feeling this.

T: You're saying that both these feelings, the good one and the painful one, can be present in the *here-and-now* at the same time?

P: For me the world has always been bad. It condemns people to suffering. That's a basic feeling that's always been with me.

T: Like a legacy?

P: That's a good expression. My father was always like this too. As if he was always fearful of something. That's what I grew up in.

T: Could we say that this feeling is out of proportion with your current life?

P: For sure! I feel we're getting close to something important slotting into place. This Weltschmerz permeates my being. It's scorched into me. It won't let me be myself. I just exist. My wife gave that as a reason when she announced she was leaving me. She can't stand it with me anymore, she said. And the fact the mood with me and around me is as if she always had to suffer, and she wanted to protect our children from that.

T: This legacy is like one that you carry sometimes with you, sometimes inside you.

P: This legacy thing is a new idea. You know, although I suffered from the divorce, at least it gave me the satisfaction of feeling there was at last a reason for this world-weariness. There was something to link it to. Until then, it was just there. Floating around. It was awful, not knowing what it was. I still don't know what it is. Definitely not the divorce. I sense this idea of legacy has triggered something inside me.

It helped Ádám greatly when he found an object for the unbearable pain. The object was his divorce. The progress came when thinking about disproportion brought up the idea of legacy. "It's not my world-weariness, but I'm carrying it too," he said later. In later phases of therapy, we explored the transmission of his father's world-weariness, and then its origin, the paternal grandmother's "archaic" trauma. The grandmother, of Jewish origin, spent several months during the Second World War terrified, in constant fear of death, in a cellar. This was the atmosphere she created in her family later, and Ádám shared this legacy. Ever since his birth he felt this deep pain, vulnerability, and often felt it was unbearable, that even death would be better.

The therapist's feelings

The transgenerational atmosphere creates a special quasi-psychotic world where one space is shared by past and present, reality and fantasy, the inner and outer worlds, the *me* and the *we*.

Often without being aware of it, the therapist may be drawn into this atmosphere. This may be through the intrusion of her own transgenerational feelings and experiences, which she is unable to handle because she finds no place for them in the work with her patient. They are difficult to interpret on the basis of transference-countertransference, and the problem brought by the patient does not warrant the quality and/or intensity of the feelings.

The transgenerational atmosphere is present in the therapy space for a long time. As a result, the transitional space, the analytic third, is weakened, or even temporarily collapses. The atmosphere's effect in certain phases of the therapy process may be varied. Perhaps it is most oppressive at the beginning of therapy, when the therapist has not yet explored what kind of psychological field she has been drawn into. She too may have transgenerational dreams, flash-like unidentifiable feelings, fears, anxieties, unwarranted somatic reactions.

Since the analyst's own involvement is as yet unidentified, just as is that of her patient, she has to contain the undigested feeling of both the analysand and herself for a long time. Containing becomes easier when the therapist manages to understand what is going on in the therapy, what phenomenon she is party to.

Second step: differentiation

An important part of analysis is when the patient begins to realize that he is a player in a transgenerational history. In this phase we begin to separate the personal *here-and-now* experience from the transgenerational stories and experiences. For Miklós in the section *The process of therapy*, this effort at separation initially posed great difficulty, and he experienced a recurrent wavering state. His basic strategy – to adapt and adjust – had worked well until he came into a conflict situation, and then he returned to a threatened state, in which he sometimes spent months. At such times he returned to the familiar transgenerational *we*-experience, which previously had provided security, to the traumatic experiences the grandparents had been through, and to their coping strategies. At such times Miklós's individual *me* became volatile, and alien. Miklós played his role, working, conducting a social life, but meanwhile inside he felt devastated.

From the we-identity to the me-identity

In the therapy process the phase of differentiation is generally protracted: the analysand recurrently brings stories that render him non-functional, paralyzed, passive. The reaction is determined by the dual presence, as if a phantom experience were controlling the reaction in the *here-and-now*. The behavior and reaction to the stories derive not from the present, but from the transgenerational legacy. An important change in this process is when the patient comes to see that he is able to identify the transgenerational atmosphere, but is not yet free in his reactions. As the *me* gathers strength, and the individual gives himself permission to start the reactions *"from the me"* as it were, the state stabilizes, though the guilt familiar from the *we*-identity is still present. For instance, when in a workplace conflict, Miklós, instead of disappearing (as he had done previously), stood his ground, then felt that if he had been present with his old fear and numbness, the managers would have been more satisfied with him. He simultaneously experienced maltreatment as a natural part of his life, while he also saw that this need not necessarily be the case.

In this differentiation phase it must constantly be borne in mind that hitherto security and continuity for the *me* has been ensured by the *we*-self, and it is important for the analysand to return to this security from time to time. We must strive not to deprive the analysand of the *we*-security until the construction and reinforcement of the *me* is able to give new security.

Reality and fantasy in the differentiation phase

In all phases of transgenerational trauma therapy, great attention must be paid to working with reality. The differentiation phase is decisive because it is through it that the patient comes into contact with his own feelings in the *here-and-now*. Alongside the experience hitherto lived via the *we*-identity (the reality of the past) a formative independent self-experience also appears. For a while this happens in parallel. The patient starts to perceive the disproportion of his emotional reactions (the reality of the external world), but at the experiential level the typical emotional reactions are those coded through the atmosphere (reality of the past). In the differentiation phase, there is the realization that actually the boundaries are not clear. Following this the differentiation of inner and outer reality can begin, and that of reality and fantasy, of past and present. The rehabilitation of fantasy helps to differentiate damaged perception, reality, and imagination.

The therapist's feelings

In the therapy process the patient and therapist experience together a growth in independence and a failure to grow. For the therapist, it is often not the repeated failure that brings a burden, though it is not easy to experience it over and over, but the depth of failure. The patient seriously disintegrates, and is almost completely devastated. As if he didn't exist. He falls to pieces. He makes the present, past, and future null and void. His relatedness to the therapist ceases. This may shock the therapist even if she has experienced this state with several patients and expects it.

Third step: between two worlds, the period of heel-kicking

There is an important period when the sufferer of transgenerational trauma behaves not in a manner determined by the *we*-experience, but the security provided by his own self has not yet formed. This is a vacuum period in the therapy process. At this point the individual feels as if he has lost his identity: the person he is, the way he is present, is not him. It is no longer him and not yet him. It is an unfamiliar, new, not self-identical, vulnerable state. He cannot now return to the old way of being, but he is present in the new one only for certain moments.

In this phase we often see that the analysand jumps with gusto into the new way of being, trying out the new identity, but after a conflict or frustrating experience he returns to the earlier *we*-state. Here he hides his injury while outwardly his attitude is one of adaptation or disappearance. Miklós put this as follows:

> "I'm kicking my heels in the doorway of the self-identical life. I dare not go in, or if I do, I dare not stay there for long. As soon as the opportunity comes, I start to work against it. I calm down when I return to the old state. At least it's familiar."

For the individual born into the transgenerational atmosphere the self-identical life is both seductive and terrible: too much about it is unknown. Also typical is the fear that if he creates something that becomes important to him, to which he is attached, it can disappear in a moment.

Miklós says: "The terrible thing is that I feel I wouldn't be able to protect it. This thought paralyzes me again and again. It keeps me here, kicking my heels in the anteroom to a self-identical life."

The new, unfamiliar way of being is still frightening, so it is a difficult and long process to build an independent identity. In the "kicking heels" phase the heir repeatedly starts out to draw the boundaries, then over and over returns to the atmosphere that provides security. This goes on until the core self is strong enough for the individual to withstand the guilt, the solitude, and until then the "Kelemen the Mason" effect holds sway. The therapist must respect this phenomenon, because if she insists on separation and over-forces independence, this might backfire. The heir can defend himself with resistance, and this may become an obstacle to change. To get over this period it may be of great help to create together what is known as a safe place.

Safe place

In the transitional phase the patient may return to the *we*-experience after an event, feeling, a flash of memory, or a grievance. The depth he goes to might vary; it may appear as absence, alienation, fear, or pain. In this state the patient sometimes instinctively finds an inner symbolic place, fantasy, or memory that provides security. The appearance of the inner symbolic place can be considered as an attempt to correct the transitional space.

For instance, Miklós, in an early phase of the intermediary state, when he disintegrated, fantasized for himself a gray room, where he could experience being safe. The enclosing walls protected him. The room had a small door, and only he had the key. After a while, the safe experience he had there gave him strength to return to the world. In a later (still transitional) phase of the therapy, Miklós no longer reacted to conflict situations by disintegrating. In one case for instance, he experienced deep, almost unbearable pain. Then he had the idea of reading his favorite poem over and over.

As we saw in the excerpt from this case, the analysand himself is able to find an inner safe place. But if this is not created spontaneously, the analyst can give a helpful nudge to its creation. In our experience, once the safe place has been created, after a conflict situation the analysand returns not to the transgenerational *we*-state, but to the corrective, *we*-place in relationship to a good object.

Reinforcing the therapist's role as an external self-object

Another important mission in this phase is to assist in the development of the self – to reinforce the individual's own core self. The therapist's role is to facilitate the escape of the individual's own trapped self from the enclosed world (from the atmosphere), and to assist the differentiation of his own and the transgenerational self-experiences. The freeing of his own self from the atmosphere helps to lead the individual back to the real world. The therapist becomes a reference person: the patient begins to perceive the real world through the therapy relationship, and begins to experience the place of external relationships and experiences in his new internal construction. In this phase the therapist creates the new milieu which helps the analysand to build this different kind of self-perception, this experiencing of emotions and moods, supportive self-reflection, a more spontaneous, creative behavior. The analysand often grows uncertain if he is on the right track – as does the therapist. The experience of having a dual way of being is similar to what an analysand experiences in other (classical) analytic processes. The difference in this case is the depth of transition and the continual presence of the guilt that accompanies change, the sense of threat associated with change. In this phase we have to deal separately with guilt, because if we do not work it through, it may become a serious obstacle to change.

Guilt is a constantly present experience, carried in the atmosphere, which may gather strength if the *we* feels under attack. At the same time, with the strengthening of the personal self, some split-off elements, such as aggression, mortal fear – may enter the consciousness, and overwhelm the *me*. A strenuous process may move towards integration, but the influx of destructive, still undigested contents may bury the *me*, slow it down, and hamper development and growth.

Containing and mirroring

In this phase of therapy one difficulty may be that as the *me* separates more from the *we*, the *me* deprived of the *we* experiences unbearable loss and emptiness. When the patient begins to build himself, he seeks his identity: like a small child at the beginning of self-construction, it is here that it dawns on him what he will be like.

One of the therapist's tasks is holding/containing: together with the patient she must contain the loss which appears as he moves further away from the *we*-identity, and also help manage the absence for the patient of his own autonomous feelings and experiences. Another task of the therapist relates to mirroring: the change may start with the therapist not mirroring the surreal world. The patient is not yet relating to reality, but has come to feel that the surreal world is not the only way of being. With time, as the patient is gradually more receptive, the therapist is able to mirror reality, the reality of the *here-and-now* relationship.

When she came to therapy with me, Tamara said that she had already been in therapy for several years, in which she had processed the family's transgenerational history and her own past. When the therapist asked why she wanted to come to therapy again, she said that her partner relationships repeatedly failed, and she wanted to change this.

She described herself to the therapist perfunctorily, without any emotional involvement, as a third-generation survivor. Her grandmother had returned from Auschwitz weighing forty kilos, practically dead. Her grandmother almost never spoke of this experience. Instead of words, she showed the terror she must have experienced with her behavior. She was very jealous of her children and grandchildren.

Tamara laid down a strict framework for our work together. She said: let's not disturb the painful past. Let's not open the wounds. The therapist sensed that with this she was showing the world in which she grew up, where family experiences and events were transmitted not by narrative, but via other channels, through the atmosphere.

Meanwhile she recreated the traumatization. Over and over she started new relationships, then repeatedly found that they did not bring redemption, and again and again she experienced loss and loneliness, being without a partner.

At the same time Tamara did not reach closure in these relationships. It was as if she lived on in them, without the reality of the relationship. In her world, parallel stories seemed to take their course in one psychological field. The therapist felt he couldn't find the path to this inner world of Tamara's, and for a time he could not. Her pain and loneliness were very deep and distant.

After a while they both sensed that in spite of the great effort made, Tamara's situation wasn't changing. The therapist expected that she would carry forward the experiences they had discussed and understood into real life; instead she started every session by saying: "Nothing's changed. Why would it, when after all nothing happens in the sessions."

Following this, the sessions continued with the therapist recalling for Tamara all they had talked about, and where they had apparently got to. It was as if the therapist had become Tamara's memory.

At the same time, it wasn't only Tamara who was forgetting what happened in the previous session, but the therapist too. He felt as if their real relationship had disappeared. Sometimes he had to make a great effort to summon up what had happened, so he endeavored to take detailed notes. On the basis of this he became aware that Tamara seemed to disappear for him in the periods between the sessions. As if something was built up between them in the session, but in the intervening time it disappeared. He decided to share this with her, and speak to her of the "Kelemen the Mason" effect.

Tamara reacted very intensely to this. She stirred in her chair. First, she turned pale as a ghost, then she blushed.

T: What's going on inside you?
P: I don't know, but I feel I'm going to sink from shame. (The clock struck.) I'd better go. I don't know, after this (pause) it will be difficult to come to the next session.

The therapist asked her to bring along this feeling of shame to the next session, because this sharing of experience had clearly had a deep effect on her.

Tamara came to the next session with a list. "I never dare give feedback on what I feel with another person," she began. "Now I've written down what feelings I had about you." While she spoke, the therapist sensed how anxious she was. He felt she was now doing something she had never done before. He could see she was scared of what reaction she would get from him. Item by item, she had to gather her strength in order to continue. She needed the therapist's encouragement.

All her life Tamara had learned not to oppose her parents, not to cause problems. Not to say what was going on inside her. She experienced this in her partner relationships too. At the beginning the relationship always went well, because she guessed her partner's every wish. When she wanted someone to care for her too, time and again she was disappointed. Then she was overtaken by a feeling of deep loneliness, desertion, which she felt she could not show.

This is what Tamara experienced in therapy too. After the initial honeymoon period she felt that even the therapist could not resolve the deep loneliness which she had carried, unidentified, since her birth.

Tamara lived not in reality, but in the *we*-world of her grandparents' legacy. The therapist's sharing of his experience brought an unexpected development. Perhaps it was not what he actually said, but the fact they could talk about their relationship. This sharing of experience established a new relationship model, where feelings and attitudes could be uttered. The therapist and the therapy relationship thus enabled the patient to relate differently to the other.

As we saw with Tamara, the idea of what I will be like after I let go of the *we*-identity prompts serious anxiety. Can I accept myself? How will I relate to the self that I become? This is why a new contract is important, as it permits the analysand to become acquainted with these fears and anxieties.

A new contract

After the *we*-identity has been brought into consciousness, the heir differentiates between his own experience the elements transmitted in the *we*-identity by the person carrying the transgenerational trauma, and what he experiences in relation to that person. In the psychotherapy process the difference steadily becomes clearer, and the two life-worlds gradually separate. As the *we*-identity becomes differentiated, more space can be given to the construction of the *me*.

In this phase of therapy, we have experienced the operation of a particular mechanism. The patient sets out on the path to create an autonomous identity, but often "backslides", returning to the starting phase, as if she did not believe she were able to get this far, or rather, as if this vision of the future were not self-identical. Time and again there is the question: is this really what she wants?

For this very reason, it may be important for the therapist to make a new contract, to set a new therapy goal with the second- or third-generation patient for the construction of a healthier, more autonomous *me*. This is decisive because we have found that the opportunity for this has hitherto been limited, or even prohibited. The parent may experience the quest for autonomy as betrayal and desertion, and by transmitting this to the child, either consciously or unconsciously, the parent blocks the path to independence.

The new contract is an important basis for further cooperation. It is an alliance in which a decisive step forward is the acknowledgment of obstructive resistance, fears, and anxieties. It is indispensable to win inner permission from the patient, so that the process of constructing autonomy can be more effective. The following excerpt from a case demonstrates this:

Cecília, a third-generation survivor, felt that her mother had died because of Cecília's efforts to become independent, so for a long time after her death she punished herself, and retained the *we*-identity. She felt that her fate was still to suffer, to live in anxiety and fear.

Differentiating the *we*-identity, i.e. acknowledging the atmosphere of the mother's trauma, opened the way to construction of the *me*, a more autonomous existence. During their work together Cecília and the therapist experienced the dynamic we earlier called the "Kelemen the Mason" effect. Cecília enthusiastic-ally set about building and things went well, but then she backslid into the initial state, the self-tormenting *we*-identity. They found that time and again Cecília withdrew her permission to move into a happier, more liberated existence.

At this point they decided to make a new contract. They clarified what inhibited construction, progress, the adherence to the new.

The contract has a symbolic meaning; it expresses that an old phase of life has come to an end and a new one is beginning. Through this the patient can experience the support of what is intact. The new vision of the present is formed, which expands the hitherto confined habitat. The new identity brings a new approach to life, perception, emotional experience, attitudes, and relatedness. The previous "threatened victim" attitude to life may be replaced by a more positive one. The patient gives himself permission for an independent life, a more joyful way of being present. The new contract seems to open up the world, allowing for an expansion in the patient's living space. A new contract is needed also so that what is created is not a new *we*-experience, but the solid beginnings of a new *me*-experience.

The therapist's feelings

In the phase of "heel-kicking" the therapist unfamiliar with the phenomenon may easily feel that his work is in vain. He may become impatient. He may hasten a process for which neither the patient nor his environment is ready. This may be reinforced by the impatience of the analysand, ascribing the lack of a permanent change to a poor level of cooperation.

Perhaps this is the period when the atmosphere reaches the therapist most; in him, as in the patient, there may appear almost uncontainable feelings of anxiety, loneliness, and emptiness. The deep undigested contents may over-whelm the therapist, who as protection may be prone to react with enactment (Bass, 2003; Feldman, 2015). In actual fact the more frequent appearance of enactments is of great significance: it signals to the therapist that something important is happening in the therapy space. In Tamara's case this occurred when the therapist began to take more frequent and detailed notes. The "role" of the notes in this case was most likely to protect against emptiness.

Fourth step: strengthening the me

In this phase of therapy, the focus is on the reinforcing of the *me*. We work in parallel with the *me* and the *we*, with feelings and experiences related to per-sonal life events and transgenerational ones, and with transference and transgenerational transference. A prerequisite for the reinforcement of the *me* is that the transgenerational experiences become symbolized and conscious. As it gathers strength, the *me* handles and integrates the transgenerational atmosphere better and better, and retreats less and less to the transgenerational *we*-experience that previously provided security. Another decisive change is the acknowledgement and experience of the difference between the two life-worlds. The constant support of the therapist and the differentiation of experiences and feelings between the two worlds assists in strengthening and stabilizing the *me*.

An early sign of progress is when the strengthening *me* allows in the feelings and behaviors that were hitherto prohibited. There is even space for extreme behavior, similar to that of a teenager testing the self boundaries.

Miklós, whose parents were forcibly relocated (see the section *The therapy process*) and thus left as a legacy the need for a high degree of adaptation, avoided every conflict and concealed his grievances deep down. Instead of having emotional reactions, he annihilated himself: this was how he protected himself from an outburst of aggression accumulating within him. In this phase of his therapy he made up for all of this: he felt that the world was a dreadful place, that he was being persecuted, and because of this he became hostile, which he expressed in almost all of his relationships. He felt anger, rage, and avoided encounters. Through his projected persecution he felt almost all his relationships to be abusive. At the same time, because he was developing awareness due to therapy, he did not allow everything to cave in around and inside of him. He was able to bring these expressions of aggression into the therapy. He could talk about them and in the therapy space he could feel them. But it was a long time before he saw that though he was persecuted, he was also a persecutor. In the security of therapy, he felt that the "dirt" (his choice of word) that he had so far repressed was overwhelming him. This inchoate awareness of his psychotic-level experience contributed greatly to his beginning to construct an authentic *me*. His experiences were no longer present in a split-off, alienated form and he began to relate to them.

The reinforcement of the *me* sets off a change in perspective such that the individual becomes able to perceive himself, to pursue his desires, to identify how he wishes to be in a relationship and in the world. In order to implement all of this, the *me* needs to be constantly present in its strengthened state.

At this point the analysand has a clearer picture of his capacity to harm and abuse himself too. The second-generation traumatized person often punishes himself because he feels he was the reason for his parent's unhappiness (and the parent thinks this too). The idea of becoming autonomous, of separation, and the onset of anger calls forth self-punishment, and this paralyzes the separation process. This can be resolved only with the help of a strong *me*. In this phase of therapy, the analysand will be strong enough to withstand the pressure caused by the replacing of the *we*-identity. He is able to bear the guilt, which restricted his autonomy and deprived him of his (own) free decisions.

Miklós had to submit his degree thesis. He didn't have much time to prepare it so he told his wife he'd have to work hard for four days. She took offense and marched off, obviously angry and disappointed. Earlier on, Miklós would have dealt with this situation very badly. He would have showered his wife with gifts to atone for his "mistake", and attempt to create a conflict-free state (though one of subjugation), and this would have entailed self-sacrifice, and self-loathing. This time, however, he bore the burden of his wife's emotional withdrawal, and did not strive to make amends. Although he felt guilt, he was able to contain it, to bear it. He no longer felt that he alone was guilty and responsible for his wife's anger. He felt, and to his own surprise, actually said that his wife was behaving selfishly, and was not being empathic. He encountered his own anger and aggression not delayed, not transferred, but in the *here-and-now*, and this frightened him. Still, he felt he was energized by it, and became stronger.

Working with reality and fantasy

As the *me* grows stronger the individual becomes able not only to consciously differentiate reactions, but to be present emotionally in a different way. This actually means a new attitude, and time is needed for the patient to be able to live with it. The continuous sense of threat lessens, and real desires, feelings, and relations emerge. It is no longer the transgenerational transference that governs the relation with the outside world, but the *me* constructed by the patient's own self, and the reality of the world perceived by it.

This process is aided by the rehabilitation of fantasy. There can be room for fantasy – the *as-if* reality – when the patient can differentiate the reality of the past from the reality of the present, and is able for relatively long periods to remain in the reality of the present. In this phase of transgenerational trauma, the individual can imagine, and can experience through rehabilitated fantasy the desired self-identical vision for the future. Through the dialogue about this the therapist can form an image of the patient's desired future fantasy, albeit permeated with fear, which they can later further build on together.

Zoltán was calm and balanced at the Tuesday session. By the Thursday session he had changed completely. His voice was shaking, his face showed despair. His thinking was narrowed. He said he felt that he didn't love his wife. He wanted to leave the relationship. He felt his wife was suffocating him with her behavior. When we went over what actually happened, it transpired that Zoltán had to submit a manuscript that he didn't have ready in time, and he had other tasks waiting to be done. This frustrating situation set off a familiar process which, in spite of his having often experienced it before, affected him as a very threatening situation. His wife, who sensed the change, in order to help became much more active, a rescuer. Zoltán experienced this as aggression, and felt it was unbearable for him. He wanted to escape from the constraint he felt. At this point, he sensed it was familiar to him. That's why he took no action. He consciously restrained himself, so as not to hurt his wife.

> He said: "I felt that what I'm feeling, the way I'm living out this situation, is exaggerated. I remembered that we have already spoken about this. I consciously delayed my reaction. I hoped that if I brought it to the therapy session, we'd understand what's going on inside me at times like this."

From a stable state, Zoltán suddenly becomes frustrated, which he shares with his wife. His wife, concerned for her husband, tries insistently to help. Zoltán suddenly finds himself in an atmosphere that he experienced with his mother. He relates to his wife through the atmosphere, perceiving her as oppressive, possessive, aggressive. At the same time, he feels he cannot hurt her, that he cannot say what he feels. He wants to escape.

With Zoltán we clarify that he wants to escape from this destructive situation. We also identify that the *me* who escapes like this, who experiences this sense of threat, feels motherly possessiveness to be dangerous. This is not attached to his wife, but is ascribed to her. Zoltán also concedes that the real relationship with his wife is far from being this threatening.

The differentiation of *we* and *me* enabled him to understand and re-align the transgenerational transference.

The therapist's feelings

In this phase of therapy in place of the earlier emptiness there may be intensive, often overwhelming feelings and fantasies. Aggression, a sense of persecution, and being threatened, may appear in the therapy space. Then mourning can also appear: with the strengthening of the *me* the *we* must be relinquished: this state is very similar to the early symbiotic existence, which the patient and therapist have created together. This is a shared loss. At the same time, the experience of processing grief is also shared, and this allows for the development of the ability to mourn.

As greater space is given to the patient's own self-sensations, there appear new countertransference feelings in the therapist. The transgenerational atmosphere and the transgenerational transference and countertransference subside. More emphasis is given to unique personal life-events and to the transference-countertransference field in the classic sense, reflecting early relationships. The transitional space (or playground) of the therapy gradually becomes more colorful, more vivacious, varied, and full – of the individual's own self-feelings.

Fifth step: re-relating to the pre-trauma family identity

In the previous phase, the focus was on strengthening the *me*. In parallel with this we worked with the *we*-experience, i.e. the legacy of the transgenerational trauma.

The strengthening *me* makes it possible to expand the psychological field narrowed by the trauma. When the *me* escapes from the atmosphere of transgenerational trauma, the heir may discover the world before the laying down of the transgenerational legacy. This may have countless benefits for second- and third-generation survivors.

For the heir who so far has experienced continuity predominantly in relation to the parent's trauma, here he has an opportunity to exit from the captivity of trauma space-time, and get to know in a new way the history of the family, events, and other episodes. Continuity is given a new meaning. The reality of the past becomes past, and reality can connect to the present. With these changes, the future can become more open, no longer controlled and distorted by the trauma.

The history and experiences of the heir fit into the family history in their own right, differentiated from the *we*; they link up to but do not merge with the history and life-world of the previous generations. The family history, which is defined not by the trauma alone, may be reconstructed.

Lia, 38 years old and single, sought the help of a psychologist because she could not form a long-term relationship. After a couple of months with her partners, either they left her or she left them.

All of the relations of Lia's grandparents were killed in the Auschwitz death camp. Lia spent many weeks with her grandparents, months even during the summer, and they told her much about their relatives who had been killed.

During analysis Lia encountered the repressed fears that her grandparents' stories had elicited in her. Because of the stories of the children who disappeared (because she didn't know exactly what happened or why), she constantly feared that one day she herself might disappear too. It also disturbed her that her grandparents suggested that the children had disappeared, but somehow were still about somewhere, so vivid was the way they spoke about them.

In analysis it became clear that the relationship between the grandparents, parents, and Lia as an only child was very strong: "In our family everyone is unhappy, as if it were not permitted to be happy," she said in one session.

When her *me* grew stronger in psychoanalytic treatment, Lia started to research her family tree. She discovered what respectable careers her ancestors had carved out, the considerable fortune they had earned, and how well they managed it, which greatly inspired her. By coming into contact with the pre-trauma family past, she gained a much stronger identity, which reinforced the *me*. Through the stronger *me* she sought opportunities to realize herself. She gave herself space and time, with patience and inner support. The reconnection with the time prior to the trauma of the transgenerational legacy sparked off a chain reaction in her life, which opened the way to new prospects for self-realization.

Continuity, space-time reparation

An important task in this phase is to correct the trauma space-time, to create instead of the trauma-centered continuity a *me*-narrative-based continuity, determined not by the *we*-experience, but by the *me*-experience. The family history is part of the *me*-experience: both the trauma and the pre-trauma period. As past becomes past, space is freed up for the experiences of the present: continuity is now based on linear time, not on the circular space-time of trauma.

During therapy, in the transitional phase with the strengthening of the *me,* the continuity of new, present relationships is already forming, but anxiety has not disappeared. Perhaps it will never disappear completely, but the proportion of it will change. This is a new experience and time is needed to integrate it. It needs to be built and brought to life. This relationship continuity is an important element of the *me*-identity: if the relationship is continuous, then so am I, so is the *me*.

In this phase anxiety may increase, because difficult feelings such as shame, pain, mortal fear, aggression, which were split off in the first generation, may appear as part of the integration process, as the *me* grows stronger – initially as an oversized, undifferentiated mass. The task of the growing *me* is to tolerate, differentiate, and name these feelings.

Zoltán, identifying with his mother, felt he had no right to live. For him, continuity meant a death-wish, and disappearance, as family members had disappeared in the war. The death-wish and disappearance represented the continuous link to those lost: everlasting remembrance. For Zoltán, in therapy, a new form of relating began to take shape to the living, for instance to his wife. This was a new, unfamiliar way of being for him, and involved him accepting that I connect, and he does not disappear, and *I* do not disappear either. For this, he needed the security that the connection of *me* was not now "fatal": it would entail no danger either to him or to others. It is a good feeling, but we have to learn to stay connected with another person.

Sixth step: integration

The aim of the last phase of the therapy is to create self-integration. The *me* that previously functioned as a split-off self-part creates an independent core self, so it is no longer the *we*-core self that gives security and continuity. The strengthened me becomes able to tell the difference between itself and the *we*. It is able to sense feelings and experiences and integrate them into the self-narrative. The continuity of the self is no longer provided by the *we*, but by the *me*. Thus, the patient becomes capable of functioning differently, based on integration, instead of the earlier functioning dominated by splitting; the split-off personal parts of the self, and the differentiated and now symbolized transgenerational self-parts are now reintegrated. Although the traumatic history belongs to the traumatized person, the experience belongs to the heir too. For instance, Miklós did not live through the forced relocation, but he felt the shame, the humiliation, the exclusion, and the stigmatization. That belonged to him too. He created this atmosphere time and time again in his own life too. The experience of being persecuted had defined his existence and the construction of his personality.

In the last phase of therapy Miklós had relinquished the detaining, clinging *we*-identity created by the grandparents. He has arrived in the present. He lives in his *here-and-now* conflicts, he is able to experience them fully, perceive them, and feel them. He has an autonomous core self, so his attitude to the legacy of his grandparents and parents is like his attitude to the real relationship he had with them. At the same time, he recognizes that the decades spent in duality have made him strong and have broadened the boundaries of his life-world.

In therapy we strive during integration for the *me*-experiences and the *we*-experiences to be integrable, for them to fit into a coherent self-narrative. After the patient identifies the atmosphere in which she has grown up, she will be able to understand how the *we*-identity, which previously provided continuity, relates to the *me*-identity, which provides a new continuity. Recognizing and differentiating the *we*-identity helps the differentiation of the individual's identity too: the individual's experience, perception, decisions, and behavior are still influenced by the *we*-identity, but the continuity, the "fundamental tone" is now given by *me*, and the path opens to a new kind of relatedness.

Because transgenerational trauma draws the heir in from her birth (conception), its effect touches on every level of perception and feeling. The legacy has an influence not only on the narrative, but as we have seen, at a somatic and visceral level, and is part of the personality. An important task from the differentiation phase is to work on differentiating the visceral feelings associated with our personal early relationships from the visceral feelings transmitted by the atmosphere (such as the differentiation of the origin of anxiety). In the integration phase we work on accepting our feelings as our own, for the differentiated somatic feelings – even they are a legacy – to be self-identical and for them to find their place in the self-narrative.

Recasting relationships

As we have seen, the *we*-identity fundamentally defines the attachment of those who live in the transgenerational atmosphere to one another. This mutual bond is generally as strong and intertwined as in conjoined twins, as we saw earlier. This often means that their lives do indeed depend on one another. If the successor wishes to exit from this bond, she must be prepared to accept that the parent might die from it. István, 40 years old, shared the following in a psychodrama group with his peers:

> I was 18 years old when I finished secondary school. I had to decide where to study next. I could have decided to go to university in a town near my parents. However, I felt I could now escape from the cloying, suffocating world in which I lived. I deliberately chose a university far away. Now I know by doing that, I killed my parents. My father died that year, and my mother not long after. Sometimes I feel that this is my crime. At other times, I feel I couldn't have done otherwise."

In the last, final phase of therapy the main task is to rework the important relationships. In addition to the relationship with the parents, the relationships with the partner, children, friends, and co-workers need to be recast. It should be borne in mind that often the choice of partner is made through the *we*, thus the partner fits and is involved in the atmosphere. To support the needs of the strengthening *me*, a goal might be for a new, more equal, more autonomous relatedness to form.

The strengthening of the *me* and the reintegration process provokes the relationship with the original family members involved in the *we*. While in the *we*, the atmosphere is rather rigid, and very probably unable to change, the *me* is already able to react flexibly and to imagine relationship alternatives. Mapping out alternatives is an important part of concluding the therapy.

In the integration phase the patient, in accordance with his autonomous self, has his own desires and expectations, which he now experiences as a natural concomitant to a relationship. He can handle any guilt that may arise. He is able to work through the earlier relationship patterns. He has greater freedom and scope for action, can operate more interactively, and experiences inner support in this.

The recasting of a relationship brings genuine changes. At the same time the patient is able to relinquish relationships that are not open to being recast. An important achievement during therapy is the ability to mourn: the dominance of splits and extreme, black-and-white moods lessen, the self- and object-images grow tamer, and there is increased tolerance of anxiety and frustration. In conflict situations the patient is able to stand his ground and support himself, and thus experiences the capacity to create the kind of presence in relationships that brings a more satisfied, liberated, cooperative, happier attitude to life.

Summary

Thinking into the atmosphere helps not only in understanding psychological processes, but also broadens the space for methodological changes. The new theoretical approach helps us to interpret differently the negative therapeutic reaction familiar in transgenerational trauma therapy: reactions previously interpreted as resistance, are given a new meaning, and fit into the therapeutic process. The theoretical approach to transgenerational trauma and the therapy recommendations based on it are fundamentally psychoanalytic in their approach, and based on psychoanalytical principles. Perhaps the most fundamental theoretical difference with the classic approach is that the new approach considers not only experiences and feelings based on personal experience, but also alien, inherited experiences; in other words, it puts emphasis on group processes and the social context. Treating experiences and feelings as alien does not mean splitting them off – on the contrary, by making them conscious they may become integrable. Later they do not haunt subsequent generations as a phantom, but as a painful, personal memory, that is part of the past. Thus, the generations slowly regain the space to live on their own terms, and to build their own identity.

Closing thoughts

The theoretical framework of the transgenerational atmosphere builds on many earlier theories and practical observations on the topic of transgenerational trauma. Within this framework we can interpret the trauma's effect on the first generation, the transmission mechanism, the effect on subsequent generations, and therapy observations.

Compared to the traditional analytic approach the transgenerational atmosphere places great emphasis on group-level processes. Relying on the theoretical basis of object-relations theories, modern theories of self, and the intersubjective schools, with the idea of the atmosphere we are envisaging an expanded psychological space, which interprets the interpersonal space or parent-child, patient-therapist interaction more broadly, expanded to a whole community, to several generations, both in cross-section and longitudinally.

It is not simply a case of dealing more with the effects of the social context and the broad and narrow environment on the individual, but rather we set out from the basic principle that individual and group-level processes cannot be separated from one another at the psychological level. The group-level *we*-experiences are deeply intertwined with the individual's life-experience-based *me*-experiences, coloring or even completely remolding them. To understand psychological processes at the individual level – the *me*-experiences – we cannot ignore the *we*-experiences: the experiences of previous generations, and the shared life-world of the socio-ethnic group(s) to which the individual belongs.

The *we*-experience may be supportive in its effect, like a good enough supportive parent: it allows the *me* to realize itself, to create its own identity different from the identify of others; when the *me* collapses, is shocked, for instance in a crisis or as a result of trauma, it provides security, a transitional, inner, psychological space, until self-cohesion is restored. In large social traumas the healthy containing function of the *we* is damaged, and may for a long time (far longer than the period of the trauma) take control over the *me*: several generations may merge together in a shared traumatized life-world, in which the individual, the *me*, has very little scope for action.

In general, it can be said that the more traumatic the environmental effects, the greater the chance of the group-level dynamic taking over: the damaged psychological space, the transgenerational atmosphere expands over several generations of the traumatized *we*-self and *we*-life-world. And conversely, the more secure the environment, the greater the opportunity for autonomy, for forming one's own self and identity, the more the *me* can realize itself.

At the same time, the individual's reaction to trauma (fortunately) is not predictable. Among the survivors of severe societal traumas there are many who are unbroken by the trauma, indeed they are strengthened: the *me* is not weaker, but stronger because of it. In their case often the milieu of creative work – artistic creation, science, helping professions – creates the psychological space in which they can resolve and preserve, or even build their individual identity. The creative process can be viewed as a *we*-experience, but a healthy, maintaining form thereof, which reinforces not the merging of the individual, but his independence. Artistic creation and the creative process itself are a shared psychological space in which the sufferer of trauma shares the experience in an abstract, creative way with an imaginary, receptive good object, and through creation the experience is both digested and shared.

Reflections

Júlia Hardy (Dr.), family and psychodrama psychotherapist

Family therapy has at its focus the system of relationships. The quality and style of relationships is brought to life in the therapy space between the therapist(s) and the family, and thus it is possible to sense it, examine it, and reflect upon it.

Esther Perel described two types of survivor Belgian Jewish families that returned from the camps: some of them lived in flats with the furniture covered with sheets, reducing their life energy to an absolute minimum, living almost invisibly, in grayness, with their eyes cast down, because another attack from the outer world might come at any moment. Other families lived with a fount of vitality, grasping every opportunity and teaching their children to enjoy the moment, because another round of persecution might come at any moment.

Families who have experienced persecution and trauma and been through crises either disintegrate or often close ranks: they close their external borders, while internally the borders that serve to share resources and keep the family solidarity become permeable. Individual needs become subsidiary to the higher priorities of hiding and survival. Experiences from the time of the Great Threat can be transferred from generation to generation in several ways. Family members may continue to cling onto one another (this was also supported by the post-war shortage of homes in Hungary), when extended families lived together, but like hedgehogs wanting to curl up, suffering from over-proximity. They experienced separation as "betrayal and a fatal risk". In these families every journey away, every leave-taking, entailed the constant fear of those who lose one another, that they were seeing each other for the last time. Thus every summer camp, or even every time someone set off for work, became a memento of the Holocaust, the inability to forget the compulsive hoarding of foodstuffs, with throwing stuff away forbidden, and hunger. By the time the third generation had grown up, they were born into "neither with you nor without you" relationships, at once full of love and hostile.

Murray Bowen, one of the founders of family therapy, developed the concept of self-differentiation, which he understood to be the extent to which someone is able to maintain freedom of thought in emotionally stressful situations. We develop this ability in the emotional processes in our family, when in various situations our parents draw us into their own conflicts. We usually choose a partner with the same level of differentiation. For the most seriously blurred families he used the concept "undifferentiated ego mass", where feeling, mood, and action exist almost indistinguishably in the family: it is impossible to tell whom they belong to. Here we come to the world of serious psychosomatic pathologies, or schizophrenia. In these families projection and projective identification processes impact from generation to generation. Meanwhile there takes shape a system where we see a pattern of almost collective conflict management, where personal borders, decisions, and responsibility, are lost. The individual finds themselves in a dilemma: either merge into the family, or violently tear themselves away from it. But "cut off" relationships overburden horizontal relationships, including that of with the partner or spouse. They swallow up energy like a "black hole".

The experiences during the Holocaust, deeds of courage or cowardice, even within one family can result in different roles. Self-sacrifice could become the core of identity. If the stories of successful flight are extant then they live on as "cautionary tales" according to the script theory of John-Byng Hall: children can be taught to help themselves, not to be naive, to look for a way out. I think for instance of the second-generation couple, both doctors, who couldn't conceive a child, and chose a child for adoption from a children's home: the one who escaped from the caged bed during their visit, because they saw in him the resourcefulness that might be useful in weathering the storms of life.

Genograms give a visual representation of the lost members of a family, or those who have sunk into the unconscious, who are present through their absence. Looking at genograms, and listening to family histories, in family therapy a pattern emerges that can also be classified alongside transgenerational trauma: one of a pair of siblings is "very good", while the other is "naughty", and they are treated accordingly. A 42-year-old man's brother and children were supported by the parents, while his family and child were not at all. This stark discrimination was seen in the grandfather's family too. The grandfather was born in 1944, in the ghetto, and when the father returned from forced labour he never freed himself of doubts over whether the newborn was his son. He was raised in an unheated room, and treated frigidly, while his little brother born a couple of years later had a fine time of it.

Family secrets and the way they impact on relationships are dealt with in several books by the American Evan Imber-Black. She examined how cover-ups and family secrets create subsystems around the secret, making family communication impenetrable and fragmentary. Secrets have keepers, and may give those who know them priority among the siblings, but they upset the relationship with other family members. Secrecy is most often motivated by tact, wanting to protect someone from some extreme danger. The bearer of the secret is relieved if he/she can draw someone into the sharing of the secret. Secrets are most frequently organized around a theme that does not match up to a presumed self-ideal, or is shameful, or causes ostracization, or pain. Secrets have a "sell-by date", and may lose potency after a certain time, as family therapist Klára Balogh writes. According to her, the third generation are able to confront the secret.

Iván Böszörményi-Nagy, who introduced the dimension of relationship ethics into family therapy, describes the concept of "destructive entitlement", a process in which we cannot give anything to our children other than what we received. The scale of family and human relationships is recalibrated around the story we have experienced: this is particularly true of the world of abuse or violence. In addition, helping outcasts and those in need can be seen as "gaining merit" in the "ethical ledger" of relationships.

Another interesting concept is "delegation", originating with Helm Stierlin, a friend of Iván Böszörményi-Nagy, in which he tried to describe the process based on the unconscious consensus of the family to mark out a child for a certain role or task. This may be a career, or a role in the family, even a role as a "memorial candle", a "charm", or a "consoler". Delegation is like a lead on a dog: if the child does not follow the designated path, he/she suffers in their self-esteem, and in their satisfaction with themselves.

Rita Horváth (PhD.), literary scholar and historian

Research fellow at the Simon Wiesenthal Institute (Vienna, Austria).

This book has had a great impact on me both personally and professionally. I am a literary scholar and a historian who researches large-scale historical traumas, mainly the Holocaust. My most recent research project focuses on Holocaust survivor testimonies and I aim to explore how literary methods of textual analysis can help historians to glean more, and more accurate, information from the ego-documents created by survivors.

Bakó and Zana, based upon both theoretical considerations and their own therapeutic experiences, have developed a powerful new theory and have also demonstrated its practical psychotherapeutic consequences. In addition, the theoretical and practical findings published in their book feel viscerally true for me, who grew up in a family in which almost all the members of the grandparents' and parents' generation were Holocaust survivors, and everybody was a survivor of large-scale historical traumas.

The new concepts, especially the transgenerational atmosphere and the transgenerational self-experience, which the authors developed, have fundamental implications for our understanding of Holocaust literature and analyzing survivor testimonies. For my research and also for understanding my own personal experiences, the most exciting novelty of the book is the claim that the creation of the transgenerational atmosphere is actually a form of communication. More precisely, the transgenerational atmosphere consists of a continuous, but continually thwarted, attempt to communicate the experiences of the survivors and their impact on them to their loved ones. Communication is a communal act, and the address built into this pathological, always already upset (and upsetting), form of communication is especially urgent. This concept clarifies why and how the descendants, who were completely dependent on the survivors at the beginning of their lives and, then, are bound to them by love, cannot avoid responding to this address, to this urgent invitation to communication and communal meaning-making.

Obviously, Bakó and Zana's work developed a new and invaluable clue to analyze family novels, which is important, as generation-novels have become one of the dominant genres of Holocaust literature. Post-Holocaust Jewish generation novels focus on the interrelated notions of continuity, discontinuity, and narrativity, as mythic, historical, and meta-historical times become intertwined during the quest of survivors and their offspring to salvage any kind of meaningful tradition and continuity after the Holocaust. Bakó and Zana's work sheds new light on a deeply disturbing phenomenon: that during this process, designed to counter the harmful impacts of the Holocaust, often the Holocaust itself and the ensuing void becomes the main tradition, the main heritage of the survivors and their descendants. Furthermore, the work of the authors also makes it possible to understand the puzzling aspect of literary works of art, such as Anne Michaels' Fugitive Pieces or Gábor Schein's Mordecháj könyve (The Book of Mordechai), that within families and other kinds of communities there exist various atmospheres warring and interfering with one another.

What is more, defining transgenerational atmosphere as communication makes it possible to reconceptualize the field of analyzing survivor testimony. It becomes both an ethical as well as a historiographical imperative to develop techniques in order to understand the specific pieces of information that are encoded in the always already crippled form of communication that is transgenerational atmosphere.

Dezső Németh (PhD., DSC.), cognitive psychologist

Implicit learning and representations in the brain

Transgenerational trauma and its effect on the next generations are critical in our everyday life and mental health. Psychoanalytic based theories have for decades, and still are today, investigating this topic; however, "harder sciences" such as cognitive psychology or neuroscience have not been able to grasp the mechanisms underlying the transmission of the trauma to the next generations. This transmission is invisible and unconscious, yet its effects are significant on the emotional life and behaviour of second, third, and fourth generations. The fascinating and inspiring book of Bakó and Zana investigates the transmission from a dynamic, psychoanalytic perspective. They show and brilliantly explain key notions such as transgenerational atmosphere, phantom, and crypt. The basic science (psychology and neuroscience) approach, in this particular domain, remains obscure compared to the psychoanalytic one. To fill this gap, I suggest here three basic learning and memory mechanisms that can be candidates for the transmission process from a cognitive psychology and cognitive neuroscience point of view. The three mechanisms are: 1) implicit statistical learning, 2) repetition, 3) interference.

1   Implicit statistical learning is a fundamental learning mechanism of the brain which is responsible for detecting and extracting patterns and correlations from our physical and social environment. Implicit learning is a memory acquisition mechanism performed in an incidental manner, without awareness of what has been learned or even of the learning situation. This learning mechanism plays a key role in our predictive processes. In effect, this implicit statistical learning is responsible for the extraction of the patterns and correlations in the parents' and family's communication, social, and emotional behavior. Our brain uses this information to be able to predict the parents' and family members' behaviors and acts as an adaptive mechanism to the family environment.

2   Several acts of behavior or communication repeat over and over again, sometimes on a daily basis. The repetition makes the implicitly learned material "hard" wired in the brain, resulting in a very strong and rigid representation. I suggest also that the phenomena called "phantom" in the book is an implicitly learned pattern of trauma that is transimitted down to the generations by implicit statistical learning. Previous cognitive neuroscience results found that implicit statistical learning and repetition can lead to a very strong consolidation showing no forgetting even after one year has past (Kóbor et al., 2017).

3   The book gives very good examples and in-depth analysis of situations when the actual feelings, fears, emotions, reactions are not related to reality, to the actual real-world context, but to past trauma, that happened many decades ago; trauma experienced by the grandparents for example. Most often, the implicit emotional, social, and communication patterns and sequences that came from one of the previous generations as consequences of trauma do not match with the real-world patterns and sequences. There is interference between "transgenerational atmosphere" (one of the keywords of the book) and reality. The strongly wired rigid and strong implicit representations are resistant against this interference. To change these representations (so-called rewiring) is very difficult. The interference between transgenerational emotional patterns and the real-world context, most of the time, remains implicit. One of the fascinating parts of the book is the one concerning therapy: it suggests that if the cause of the emotions such as fear and anxiety can be "pulled" from inside to the outside, the rewiring

process is more effective. This idea reflects well on principle in cognitive neuroscience: explicit instruction can boost the rewiring of automatic behaviors and reactions (Szegedi-Hallgató et al., 2017).

All in all, transgenerational trauma is a very important phenomenon not only from a clinical but also from a basic science perspective. Unfortunately it is rather neglected in cognitive psychology and neuroscience. I believe it is undeniable that learning and memory processes are at the heart of phenomena such as this one. In effect, from a brain science point of view, a deeper understanding of how trauma can be transmitted from one generation to the next, or even further, should be explored via this notion of (implicit) learning and the mechanisms that underlie it.

In parallel, the investigation of the effect of transgenerational trauma could also impart new theories and knowledge on learning and memory processes that could help us better understand these mechanisms as a whole.

Acknowledgement

Thanks to Kate Schipper for helpful comments on the manuscript.

References

Kóbor, A., Janacsek, K., Takács, Á., & Nemeth, D. (2017). Statistical learning leads to persistent memory: Evidence for one-year consolidation. *Scientific reports*, 7(1), 760.

Szegedi-Hallgató, E., Janacsek, K., Vékony, T., Tasi, L. A., Kerepes, L., Hompoth, E. A., & Németh, D. (2017). Explicit instructions and consolidation promote rewiring of automatic behaviors in the human mind. *Scientific reports*, 7(1), 4365.

András Szécsényi (PhD.), historian

Senior researcher at Jewish-Hungarian Historical Institute of Milton Friedman University (Budapest); researcher and archivist at the Archives of Corvinus University of Budapest; Bolyai János Fellow from the Hungarian Academy of Sciences.

As a historian I deal with the Hungarian aspects of the Holocaust, and my work focuses primarily on the history of the experience of the Holocaust. In reconstructing the tragic events of the past, in most cases I examine the point of view of victims/survivors, and base my writing on sources linked to them. In my view, as an increasing number of social researchers believe worldwide about our recent past, written or even oral individual reports are often more credible sources of the reality of the events than any other, although they all necessarily bear the mark of subjectivity.

When examining sources of personal stories from after the war, the signs of post-traumatic stress can usually be found. For example, in the case of the group of provincial Hungarian Jews who in 1944 experienced as adults the ghettofication, deportation, and persecution of themselves and their family members, and the men who had been drafted for forced labor, the tragic event persisted all through the remainder of their lives as a trauma in some form. There were of course primarily personal reasons for this: fear, fear of death, starvation, torture, the shock of losing one's loved ones etc. is conjured up shortly after the events occured, or sometimes after a very long time. Secondly, historical processes have actually reinforced the post-traumatization of the Shoah survivors: after 1945, the Stalinist communist dictatorship in Hungary did not allow people to live out their Jewish identity, or at least it was inadvisable. Although this situation changed after a good decade had passed, from 1956, in the decades when dictatorship softened, it was not possible to speak or write freely about the Holocaust, until the end of the 1980s. In this way, the thousands of Holocaust survivors could not speak of their individual pain, and there was no processing of it at the societal level.

I have found countless times that in the survivor memoirs written or recorded during the four decades after the war, each interlocutor tried to take on and neutralize the concepts expected by official policy: thus rather than mass murder they spoke of persecution; rather than victims they spoke of martyrs of fascism. This making light of the trauma, "assisted from above" does not in any way amount to a resolution of the trauma. On the contrary: it attaches, it is transferred to the following generation, in almost every case I know, carrying the individual trauma on. The authors of this volume describe this with the new term transgenerational trauma, a concept which, I hope, will take root not just in clinical psychology, but in social psychology and historical scholarship. In the case of transferred trauma I have many times observed how members of the second generation (the children of the survivors) have repressed their identities, out of shame, guilt, or fear of the political impact. Members of the third generation, however, thanks to the free thinking that took shape in the democratic circumstances after 1990, have chosen to talk about things, which I believe has had a positive effect on those members of the first generation still alive. In other words, in their case the trauma has become a collective memory of the family and the Jewish community. Today however, due to politics, there are once more signs of reticence, and the inherited post-traumatic experience appears to be approaching another frontier; this is generating new processes among the families of various Holocaust survivors in Hungary.

Thus the study of the trauma of the psyche is linked to that of historical-social processes. To better understand the two of them, with a broad view of society and comparison with other traumas, this volume is of invaluable assistance. It is to be hoped it will stimulate discussion in related fields touching upon this subject.

Ágnes Zana (PhD.), cultural anthropologist

Semmelweis University, Institute of Behavioral Sciences, Hungary, Budapest.

For me, this book represented a journey in self-knowledge, together with all the thrill and difficulty that entails. I wondered: what kind of social environment could the descendants of victims, perpetrators, and witnesses meet and listen to and understand one another? In the study of cultures it may seem to the researcher that the stories of human history spanning centuries, and millennia, are the stories of smaller human communities, ethnic groups, and nationalities, living side by side, unwilling or unable to understand one another.

When I was an anthropology student, I came across Mario Vargas Llosa's book *The Storyteller*, which made a deep impression on me. The Storyteller of the title lives in Amazonian Indian culture, and is the living memory of the tribe, a chosen one who has to know the history of his people, and even its stories, which must be preserved and passed on for posterity. He remembers things that in reality he cannot remember, yet he stores the joys and troubles of the old stories, living through them himself.

Reading the methodology and stages of therapy, I imagined that in a third phase of the work of therapy the therapist becomes the Storyteller, over and over conjuring up and experiencing the stories and experiences that have been told by the patient.

The transgenerational atmosphere, and the expanded self-state of the child and family members born into it – the survivors – is strongly reminiscent of the symbiotic family model of traditional Gipsy families today. Just as our limbs, hands, and feet belong to us, so the family members belong together in much stronger and more unusual emotional bonds, whose advantages and disadvantages (adaptive and maladaptive characteristics) we can experience in Western-type societies. An advantage might be the close interdependence and mutual support in difficult situations, and a disadvantage, in a majority society that works differently, might be the experience of situations which typically provoke tension in the provision of health care, or the idea/feeling that separation is dangerous.

Sleep comes to mind, and that belief world, animism for instance, existence beyond the tangible, where spirits or other beings, other levels of existence, identify the community itself and the community senses and believes that this spirit world exists. A person with any kind of transcendant belief experiences this world as perfectly real, and expands the inner reality to the outside world, and at the same time the collective reality – belief in the indidvidual – is interiorized. Thus this interior reality is also a collective reality: its operation is clear for every member of the community and its rules are to be adhered to.

The disintegration of the *we*-experience appears particularly dangerous, and again reminds me of religious belief. The questioning of faith on the part of the believer can trigger unusually powerful reactions, or tempers, representing as it does a threat to the collective belief and thus the disintegration of the *we* – the (spiritual) community that gives security and a framework. A similar taboo in monotheistic religions is the questioning of the existence or the decisions of God.

As in the transference-countertransference work there arises the feeling of a fear of death, when the patient relinquishes his customary feelings and steps outside the transgenerational atmosphere, and arrives from the *we*-self to the *me*-self – this phenomenon is reminiscent of that of voodoo death. Voodoo death is, again, a phenomenon found in descriptions of natural peoples, but also an experience that seems familiar in modern societies, when the person ostracized by the community for some (primarily moral) misdeed, withdraws and dies of ostracization, thus well demonstrating the inconceivability of existence without the community.

Later the idea took shape in me that the therapist is like a shaman. In the therapy space the past, the trauma, and the *here-and-now* appear at the same time, and the therapist perceives this at once, just like the shaman, in whom, in his trance-like state, two worlds meet, that of the living, and that of the dead, the ancestors. A privileged state, outside of time.

The process that appears in the therapeutic work, expressed in the separation of the earlier self-state as the *me*-self gathers strength, is highly reminiscent of the process that seems to be the clear direction of development in modernizing societies from the second half of the twentieth century: the phenomenon of Autonomy, in the ethical sense, born as a result of social individualization processes. The autonomous person, who makes responsible decisions about his own life, has the freedom to think, decide, and act, and in moral terms too is the ideal of the developing society. In this ideal social model the individual is capable of autonomous thinking and decisions, and community socialization has a primary role in this. In societies that operate democratically this need appears not just at the individual level, but at the society level: it is an expectation not only of the individual, but also of the community. In this model, society expects the individual to think and decide responsibly, having weighed up the interests of the individual and the community. For this, therapeutic self-knowledge is necessary, of the kind that must be realized at the level of society. This naturally requires a society to be morally mature enough to confront its own responsibility – not just at the individual level.

The patient who mourns the loss associated with the *we*-state reminds me of the rites used when a person moves to a different stage of life through a significant event in his life. For instance when a girl becomes a woman, or a boy a man, getting married, finishing studies and starting to work, having children, retirement, etc. Here too is a special kind of mourning, an ambivalent state, that may be characterized by joy and pain, a sense of loss and also fear. The individual mourns his previous life, experiences the losses, and the rites assist him in this. This way he can focus on the future, and fully experience the joys associated with the new life-task. In the transgenerational atmosphere the therapist is the outer helper for the patient, and the rites are the rites of therapy.

Reading the book helps us to understand how large social traumas can have an impact that lasts for generations, and how one or another event long since past becomes a source of continuous mourning; how individual events appear in the collective unconscious, and these events remain extant for a long time, over generations, through cultural media such as religion, tradition, and rites.

János Zana (Dr.), control systems specialist

Szent István University of Budapest. Post-secondary degree in engineering and technology discipline.

I aim to comment on the subject referred to in the title, the psychological model of the transfer of transgenerational trauma, introducing a somewhat distant specialist angle, using concepts from IT, or to be specific: telecommunications.

A theoretical and practical science, telecommunications is an essential part of IT. It deals with processes necessary for information (the message) to be transmitted from the source to the receiver.

In my notes I shall deal with the factors that disrupt the contents of the information. Of these I would highlight:

- an incomplete transfer of information, or a reduction in the transmission speed,
- the redundancy of the information,
- noise and disturbance overlaid onto the information.

I shall try to demonstrate the incomplete nature of information with a musical analogy. Let us suppose that we play a normal note, A, on a violin, viola, and cello, one after the other. Naturally the listener can distinguish between the notes on the three instruments. This can be easily explained: the fundamental tone is colored by various overtones and formants, which are higher in frequency than the fundamental tone.

Now let us consider a case in which the characteristics of the chain of sound transfer deteriorate. More and more overtones are omitted from the band of frequencies; and it becomes increasingly difficult to distinguish the instruments from one another. If the channel's capacity is limited to the extent it is able only to transmit the fundamental tone, we are unable to distinguish the sound of the instruments. We do not know whether we are listening to a violin, a viola, or a cello.

On this basis, how is the transfer of human emotions and information to be interpreted? Trauma victims recall less and less of the events that took place. The only elements to be transferred are the most important, or the ones that trigger greatest social interest. Perhaps even society itself repeats the same reports ad infinitum, which the descendants have already heard thousands of times. In this way the essential contents of the message transmitted is narrowed down, because certain parts of the information are absent. Social traumas thus seem less painful, or more terrible than in reality. The person receiving the information is given distorted information.

My second comment is related to prolixity, the redundancy of the message. In such cases the information content of the message includes repetition, and the same report is repeatedly transmitted to the target person – perhaps unintentionally.

In IT there are descriptions of the advantages and disadvantages of redundancy. In terms of the topic in hand, in regard to social relationships, we can see it only as harmful, because the flood of information smothers the essential part of the message.

My third comment is something that telecommunications terms a noisy channel. Staying with our musical analogy, this is what happens if a clarinet sounds at the same time as a violin. In this case it is more difficult to judge the quality of the violin and the skill of the player. In other words, we take on irrelevant information, which covers the contents of the actual message.

Countless examples of this can be found in society. Dictatorial societies produce distorted, incomplete versions of history. The press, the media, and historical scholars falsify the information passed on. The media highlight what is spectacular or intimidating. Historical scholarship transmits things that are essential in the eyes of either a minority or a majority, even if those practicing it are unbiased scholars, independent of the authorities. In both cases, information is distorted. Partly because a part of it is withheld. And partly because an untruth, an error, or a misunderstanding is added.

Whether we speak of communication between individuals or at the society level, if the original information is lost, or if irrelevant elements are added, the information is distorted. This is what is known as a noisy channel in telecommunications: the information that reaches the receiver is not what the source transmitted.

References

Ábrahám, M. ([1975, 1987], 2001). Feljegyzések a Fantomról – Freud Metapszichológiá-jának Kiegészítése. In: Ritter A. and Erős F. (eds.): *Válogatás magyar származású fran-cia pszichoanalitikusok munkáiból. A megtalált nyelv.* Új Mandátum, Budapest, 66–71.

Abraham, N., and Torok, M. (1984). "The Lost Object – Me": Notes on Identification within the Crypt. *Psychoanalytic Inquiry*, 4:221–242.

Abraham, N., and Torok, M. (1994). *"The Shell and the Kernel." Renewals of Psycho-analysis.* Vol. 1. Translated by Nicholas T. Rand. University of Chicago Press, Chicago.

Ajkay, K. (2016). *A bizalomtól a találkozásig.* Ed.: Kökény, V. Lélekben Otthon Köz-hasznú Alapítvány, Budapest.

Allan, G. J., Fonagy, P., and Bateman, W. A. ([2008], 2011). *Mentalizáció a Klinikai Gyakor-latban.* [Mentalazing in clinical practice] Translated by: Bulath, M. Lektorálta: Sarkadi, B. és Schmelowszky, Á. Lélekben Otthon Könyvek. Oriold és Társai Kiadó, Budapest.

Anisfeld, L., and Richards, D. A. (2000). The Replacement Child: Variations on a Theme in History and Psychoanalysis. *Psychoanalytic Study of the Child*, 55:301–318.

Bakó, T. (2005). Egy szexuális abúzus feldolgozása. *Thalassa*, 1:83–97.

Bakó, T. (2009). *Sorstörés. A trauma lélektana egy pszichoteraputa szemszögéből.* Psycho Art, Budapest.

Bakó, T. (2017). Intraszubjektivitás a traumafeldolgozásban. In: Gerlinger, L. – Kovács, P. (ed.): *Egy hajóban ... tisztelgő tanulmánykötet Riskó Ágnes születésnapjára.* Medicina, Budapest, 219–229.

Bakó, T., and Zana, K. (2015). Kölcsönös analízis Ferenczi Sándor nyomán. Átmeneti terek, átmeneti valóságok. *Imágó Budapest*, 2015, 4(4): 79–99. Retrieved from www.imagoegyesulet.hu/tartalom.php?kategoria=46&azonosito=163

Bakó, T., and Zana, K. (2017). Transgenerational Trauma Re-captured and Re-interpreted by Means of a Mutual Analysis, the Impossibility of Remembering. Translated by George Sagi in: Feldman, J. M., Nosek, L., Bakó, T., O'Neil, R., and Zana, K. (eds.): *Haunted Intimacy: International Perspective on Holocaust-Related Trauma and Ghosts in Analyst Analysand.* 29 July 2017. IPA 50th and IPSO 24th Congress, Buenos Aires.

Bakó, T., and Zana, K. (2018). The Vehicle of Transgenerational Trauma: The Transge-nerational Atmosphere. *American Imago*, 75(2):271–285.

Balint, M. (1979). *The Basic Fault: Therapeutic Aspects of Regression.* Tavistock Publications, London – New York.

Bálint, M. (1999). *Elsődleges Szeretet És Pszichoanalitikus Technika I–II.* Animula Kiadó, Budapest.

Baradon, T. (Ed.). (2010). *Relational Trauma in Infancy: Psychoanalytic, Attachment, and Neuropsychological Contributions to Parent-infant Psychotherapy.* Routledge, London.

Bárdos, K., Bárkán, Gy., Fülöp, M., Halmai, J., Hoyer, M., Kelemen, A., Krausz, É., László, K., and Virág, T. (1995). *Magyar Emlékmécsesek.* Tanulmányok a KÚT pszichoter-ápiás rendelő gyakorlatából: holokauszt túlélők és leszármazottaik terápiája. Ed. László K. Magatartástudományi füzetek 4. SOTE Magatartástudományi Intézet – MAPET – Vége-ken Alapítvány, Budapest.

Bass, A. (2003). "E" Enactments in Psychoanalysis: Another Medium, Another Message. *Psychoanalytis Dialogues,* 13:657–675.

Bezoari, M., and Ferro, A. (1989). Listening, Interpretations and Transformative Functions in the Analytical Dialogue. *Rivista Di Psicoanalisi,* 35(4):1014–1050.

Bezoari, M., Ferro, A., and Politi, P. (1994). Listening, Interpreting and Psychic Change in the Analytic Dialogue. *International Forum of Psychoanalysis,* 3(1):35–41.

Bion, W. R. (1959). Attacks on Linking. *International Journal of Psycho-Analysis,* 40:308–315.

Bion, W. R. (1962). The Psycho-Analytic Study of Thinking. *International Journal of Psycho-Analysis,* 43:306–310.

Bion, W. R. ([1970], 2006). *Figyelem és érzelem.* [Attention and interpretation] Translated by Schmelowsky, Á. Lélekben Otthon Kiadó, Budapest.

Caruth, C. (1996). *Unclaimed Experience: Trauma, Narrative, and History.* Johns Hopkins University Press, Baltimore.

Civitarese, G. (2019). The Concept of Time in Bion's "A Theory of thinking". *Int. J. Psycho-Anal,* 100(2):182–205.

Cooper, A. (1986). Toward a Limited Definition of Psychic Trauma. In: Medison, R. A. (ed.): *The Reconstruction of Trauma.* Connecticut International Universities Press, Medison, 41–56.

Cserne, I., Pető, K., Szilágyi, J., and Szőke, Gy. (1989). Az Elmaradt Gyász. *Múlt És Jövő,* 1:31–32.

Cserne, I., Pető, K., Szilágyi, J., and Szőke, Gy. ([1990], 2014). Az első és a második generációs holocaust-túlélők és gyermekeik. [The Second and the Third Generation Holocaust Survivors and Their descendants.] In: Pető, K: *A csodálatos csecsemő. Pszi-choanalízis és határterületei.* Oriold és Társai Kiadó, Budapest, 213–227.

Ericson, E. A. (1963). *Childhood and Society.* Norton, New York.

Erős, F. (2017). Kísértő érzelmek: A Történelem fantomjai. *Imágó Budapest,* 6(3): 101–110.

Erős, F., Kovács, A., and Lévai, K. (1985). Hogyan Tudtam Meg, Hogy Zsidó Vagyok. *Medvetánc,* 2–3:129–179.

Faimberg, H. (2005). *The Telescoping of Generations. Listening to the Narcissistic Links between Generations.* Routledge, London.

Feldman, M. J. (2015). Ghost Stories: Transgenerational Trauma and Witnessing in Analyst and Analysand. *Psychoanalytic Dialogues,* 25(5):600–613.

Felsen, I. (2017). Adult-Onset Trauma and Intergenerational Transmission: Integrat-ing Empirical Data and Psychoanalytic Theory. *Psychoanalysis, Self and Context,* 12(1):60–77.

Ferenczi, S. (1985). *The Clinical Diary of Sándor Ferenczi.* Harvard University Press, Cambridge – London.

Ferenczi, S. ([1932], 1996). *Klinikai Napló.* Akadémiai Kiadó, Budapest.

Ferenczi, S. ([1933], 2006a). Nyelvzavar a felnőttek és a gyermek között. In: *Technikai írások*. Animula Kiadó, Budapest, 101–112.

Ferenczi, S. ([1933], 2006b). A trauma a pszichoanalízisben. In: *Technikai Írások*. Animula Kiadó, Budapest, 112–120.

Ferro, A., and Civitarese, G. (2016). Psychoanalysis and the Analytic Field. In: Elliott, A. and Prager, G. (ed.): *The Routledge Handbook of Psychoanalysis in the Social Sciences and Humanities*. Routledge, London, New York, 132–148.

Fonagy, P., and Target, M. ([2003], 2005). *Pszichoanalitikus elméletek a fejlődési pszichopatológia tükrében*. [Psychoanalytical Theories. Perspective from Developmental Psychopathology] Ed.: Bókay, A. and Erős, F. Translated by: Milák, P., Pető, K., Ratkóczi, É., Unoka, Zs. Gondolat, Budapest.

Grünberg, K., and Markert, F. (2012). A Psychoanalytic Grave walk – Scenic Memory of the Shoah. On the Transgenerational Transmission of Extreme Trauma in Germany. Translated by Walker, M.J. *American Journal of Psychoanalysis*, 72(3):207–222.

Hermann, J. (2003). *Trauma és gyógyulás*. Háttér Kiadó – Kávé Kiadó – NANE Egyesület, Budapest.

Hopper, E. (1991). Encapsulation as a Defence against the Fear of Annihilation. *International Journal of Psychoanalysis*, 72(4):607–624.

Horváth, R. (2005). A tanú szerepe: A magyar holokauszt-irodalom a világirodalomban. In: Horváth, R. (ed.): *Maamakim. Holokauszt-tanulmányok. Holokauszt a világirodalomban*. ELTE BTK, Holokauszt-tanulmányok Program, Budapest, 1:7–15.

Horváth, R., and Zana, K. (2017). "Valuable and Also difficult": At the Meeting Point of Historical and Psychological Interviews. In: Kangisser Cohen, Sh., Fogelman, E., and Ofer, D. (eds.): *Children in the Holocaust and Its Aftermath*. Historical and Psychological Studies of the Kestenberg Archive, Berghahnbooks, New York, Oxford, 81–96.

Jucovy, E. M. (1994). A Pszichoanalízis Hozzájárulása A Holocaust Tanulmányozásához. *Thalassa*, 5(1–2):12–31.

Jucovy, M. E. (1985). Telling the Holocaust Story: A Link between the Generations. *Psychoanal. Inq.*, 5(1):31–49.

Jucovy, M. E. (1992). Psychoanalytic Contributions to Holocaust Studies. *J. Psycho-Anal.*, 73:267–282.

Kernberg, O. F. (2012). Some Observations on the Process of Mourning. In: Kernberg, O. E. (ed.): *The Inseparable Nature of Love and Aggression*. American Psychiatric Publishing, Washington, DC, 243–266.

Kestenberg, J. S. (1980). Psychoanalysis of Children of Survivors from the Holocaust: Case Presentations and Assessment. *Journal of the American Psychoanalytic Association*, 28:775–804.

Kestenberg, J. S. (1994). A túlélők gyermekei és a gyermek-túlélők. *Thalassa*, 5 (1–2):81–100.

Kipper, D. (1998). Psychodrama and Trauma: Implications for Future Interventions of Psychodramatic Role Playing Modalities. *Journal of Group Psychotherapy, Psychodrama and Sociometry*, 51(3):113–121.

Kohut, H. ([1971], 2001). *A szelf analízise*. Animula Kiadó, Budapest. [The Analysis of the Self., New York, International Universities Press].

Kovács, É., Lénárt, A., and Szász, A. L. (2014). Oral History Collections on the Holocaust in Hungary. S.I.M.N.–Shoah: Intervention. Methods, Documentation, October 15,

2014: 1–18. http://simon.vwi.ac.at/index.php/working-papers/43-kovacs-eva-lenart-andras-szasz-anna-lujza

Lőrincz, Zs., Gyomlai, É., Szajcz, Á., Zana, K., and Sinkovics, A. (2019). A bioni mezőelmélet. Egy kortárs interszubjektív elmélet. [The bionien field theory. A contemporary intersubjective theory.] *Lélekelemzés*, Budapest, 197–231, 2019/2.

Lust, I. (1999). A Szubjektum kiszolgáltatottsága. Gondolatok a pszichoanalitikus kultúra – kritika feladatairól. In: Lust, I. (ed.): *Pszichoanalízis és kultúra*. Animula Kiadó, Budapest, 72–87.

Mészáros, J. (1990). Társadalmi elfojtások megjelenése a pszichoanalízisben. *Thalassa*, 1(1):31–38.

Mészáros, J. (2003). A Modern traumaelmélet építőkövei. Ferenczi paradigmaváltása a traumaelméletben. In: Juhász, A. (ed.): *A gyöngéd analitikus és a kemény tudományok*. Animula Kiadó, Budapest, 66–74.

Niederland, W. G. (1968). Clinical Observations on the "Survivor syndrome". *International Journal of Psychoanalysis*, 49(2–3):313–315.

Ogden, T. H. (2004). The Analytic Third: Implications for Psychoanalytic Theory and Technique. *Psychoanal Q*, 73(1):167–195.

Perroud, N., Rutembesa, E., Paoloni-Giacobino, A., Mutabaruka, J., Mutesa, L., Stenz, L., Malafosse, A., and Karege, F. (2014). The Tutsi Genocide and Transgenerational Transmission of Maternal Stress: Epigenetics and Biology of the HPA Axis. *World J Biol Psychiatry*. 2014 May, 15(4):334–345.

Pető, K. (1999). Identitás és történelem. In: Virág, T. (ed.): *A társadalmi traumatizáció hatásai és pszichoterápiájának tapasztalatai* (Konferencia, 1998. November 13–15.). Animula Kiadó, Budapest, 84–88.

Pető, K. (2014). *A csodálatos csecsemő. Pszichoanalízis és határterületei*. Oriold és Társai Kiadó, Budapest.

Prager, J. (2003). Lost Childhood, Lost Generations: The Intergenerational Transmission of Trauma. *Journal of Human Rights*, 2(2):173–181.

Ramo-Fernández, L., Schneider, A., Wilker, S., and Kolassa, I. T. (2015). Epigenetic Alterations Associated with War Trauma and Childhood Maltreatment. *Behav Sci Law*. 2015 Oct, 33(5):701–721.

Rand, M. ([1994], 2001). Titok és utókor – A transzgenerációs fantom elmélete. In: Ritter A. and Erős, F. (ed.): *Válogatás magyar származású francia pszichoanalitikusok munkáiból. A Megtalált Nyelv*. Új Mandátum, Budapest, 62–65.

Rosenfeld, D. (1986). Identification and Its Vicissitudes in Relation to the Nazi Phenomenon. *Int. J. Psycho-Anal*, 67(1):53.

Schwab, G. (2009). Replacement Children: The Transgenerational Transmission of Traumatic Loss. *American Imago*, 66:277–310.

Stern, D. N. (1985). *The Interpersonal Word of the Infant: A View from Psychoanalysis and Developmental Psychology*. Basic Books, New York.

Stern, D. N. (2002). *A csecsemő személyközi világa a pszichoanalízis és a fejlődéslélektan tükrében*. Animula Kiadó, Budapest.

Szilágyi, J., Cserne, I.,, Pető, K., and Szőke, Gy. (1992). A második és a harmadik generációs holocaust túlélők és gyermekeik. *Psychiatria Hungarica*, 7(2):117–129.

Szondi, L. ([1937], 1992, 1996). A tudattalan nyelvei: szimptóma, szimbólum és választás. Szondi Lipót életművéből. Thalassa, 7(2), Thalassa Alapítvány, Budapest, 96(2):61–82. Szondi Lipót: Die Sprachen des Unbewussten: Symptom, Symbol und Wahl. Eredetileg megjelent: Szondiana II., (a Schweitzerische Zeitschrift für Psychologie und ihre Anwendungen 26. számának melléklete). Jelen fordítás alapja a Szondiana 1992/2. számában megjelent újraközlés, amely jegyzeteket nem tartalmaz.

Tolcsvai Nagy, G. (2007). *Idegen Szavak Szótára.* Osiris, Budapest`.

Van Der Kolk, B. A., and Fisler, R. (1996). Dissociation and the Fragmentary Nature of Traumatic Memories: Overview. *Brit. J. Psychother.*, 12:352–361.

Vikár, Gy. (1994). Zsidó sors(ok) az analitikus rendelés tükrében. *Thalassa*, 5(1–2):139–146.

Virág, T. (1993). Kollektív trauma – egyéni öngyógyítás. In: Lukács, D. (ed.): *A Magyar Pszichoanalitikus Egyesület Tudományos Előadásai 1991–1992.* MPE – Animula Kiadó, Budapest, 23–35.

Virág, T. (1994). Kút És Műhely. A Holocaust-szindróma megjelenése a pszichoterápiás gyakorlatban. *Thalassa*, 5(1–2):129–138.

Virág, T. (1996). *Emlékezés egy szederfára.* Ed. László K. Animula Egyesület – KÚT pszichoterápiás rendelő, Budapest.

Virág, T. (1999). Soá és ősbizalom. In: Hamp, G., Horányi, Ö., and Rábai L. (ed.): *Magyar megfontolások a Soáról.* Balassi Kiadó – Magyar Pax Romana Fórum – Pannonhalmi Főapátság, Budapest–Pannonhalma, 281–284.

Volkan, V. (2013). Large-Group-Psychology in Its Own Right: Large-Group Identity and Peace-Making. *International Journal of Applied Psychoanalytic Studies*, 10(3):210–246.

Wardi, D. ([1992], 1995). *Emlékmécsesek. A holokauszt gyermekei.* [Memorial Candles: Children of the Holocaust.] Ed. Balla E. Ex Libris Kiadó.

Winnicott, W. D. (1953). Transitional Objects and Transitional Phenomena – A Study of the First Not-Me Possession. *International Journal of Psycho-Analysis*, 34:89–97.

Winnicott, W. D. (1960). The Theory of the Parent-Infant Relationship. *International Journal of Psycho-Analysis*, 41:585–595.

Winnicott, W. D. ([1971], 1999). *Játszás és valóság.* Translated by: Bíró, S. and Széchey, O. [Playing and Reality] Animula Egyesület, Budapest.

Winship, G., and Knowles, J. (1996). The Transgenerational Impact of Cultural Trauma: Linking Phenomena in Treatment of Third Generation Survivors of the Holocaust. *British Journal of Psychotherapy*, 13:259–266.

Yehuda, R., Daskalakis, N. P., Bierer, L. M., Bader, H. N., Klengel, T., Holsboer, F., and Binder, E. B. (2016). Holocaust Exposure Induced Intergenerational Effects on FKBP5 Methylation. *Biol Psychiatry.* 2016 Sep 1, 80(5):372–380.

Youssef, N. A., Lockwood, L., Su, S., Hao, G., and Rutten, B. P. F. (2018). The Effects of Trauma, with or without PTSD, on the Transgenerational DNA Methylation Alterations in Human Offsprings. *Brain Sci.* 2018 May 8, 8(5):1–7.

Zana, K., and Horváth, R. (2013). Trauma Éés szelf-narratíva: gyerek holokauszttúlélők tanúvallomásainak interdiszciplináris elemzése [Trauma and Self-narrative: Interdisciplinary Analysis of Child Survivors' Holocaust testimonies]. *Lélekelemzés*, 2:230–256.

Index

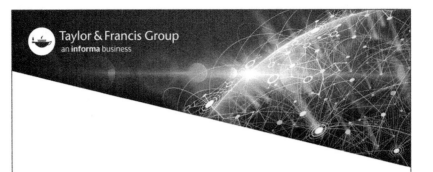